Devil's Disciple

The Deadly Dr. H.H. Holmes

Judy Miller Snavely

Bloomington, IN Milton Keynes, UK

AuthorHouse™
1663 Liberty Drive, Suite 200
Bloomington, IN 47403
www.authorhouse.com
Phone: 1-800-839-8640

AuthorHouse™ UK Ltd.
500 Avebury Boulevard
Central Milton Keynes, MK9 2BE
www.authorhouse.co.uk
Phone: 08001974150

This book is a work of non-fiction. Unless otherwise noted, the author and the publisher make no explicit guarantees as to the accuracy of the information contained in this book.

First published by AuthorHouse 5/26/2006

ISBN: 1-4259-2689-4 (sc)
ISBN: 1-4259-2690-8 (dj)

Library of Congress Control Number: 2006903081

Printed in the United States of America
Bloomington, Indiana

This book is printed on acid-free paper.

Photo Credit: Gary Patton Photography, Sand Springs, OK

This book is for Wiley and Samantha, who always believed in me. I love you guys.

ACKNOWLEDGEMENTS

A project like this one cannot be completed without running up debts to a bevy of folks for their assistance.

First of all, I owe a debt that cannot be repaid to Stephen Williams of the Better for Brian Foundation in Tulsa for all his work and sweat in getting my really sad microfilm sketches into printable condition. Also for the amazing cover art and for your friendship, Stephen, which is priceless. Thank you, thank you, thank you. I owe you more pecan pies than can be counted.

Also to Craig Nelson of Loveland Press, my thanks for all your encouragement, enthusiasm, and guidance with this project. To Teresa Hoy, who sweated blood with me for three days in a hotel room hammering out the final draft, this book would not be what it is without your help.

To Sgt. Vincent Baiocchetti of the Gilmanton, N.H., Police Dept., for his time in showing me around the birthplace of the amazing Mr. Mudgett/Dr. Holmes; to Cheryl Pince, Supervisor of Special Collections at the Abraham Lincoln Presidential Library in Springfield, IL, for permission to reprint the marvelous sketches from your archives; same for the Free Library of Philadelphia for access to the archives of the Philadelphia Inquirer; to the Local History Collection of the Central Fort Worth Public Library and to the Tarrant County Courthouse Clerk who helped me find the Fort Worth deed; to the Harold Washington

Library Center of the Chicago Public Library; and to Rex Tomb, Unit Chief of FBI Public Affairs in Washington, for your assistance in finding me a profiler's ear. And special thanks to the folks at the Library of Congress for helping secure copies of Dr. Holmes' memoirs and the amazing case study of Mudgett/Holmes by Federal Criminologist Arthur MacDonald.

To all the folks who read this manuscript and gave me feedback: to Odell and Carla Jordan, dear friends and cheerleaders; to Claudean Erdner, Jeannie Harrison, and Kathy Bradley. But again, most especially to the two people in my life in whom I could always trust the manuscript for a (sometimes painfully) honest critique, Samantha and Wiley. And to my top research assistant, again husband Wiley, for all you do for me. I love you.

To Dachshund Extraordinaire, Oscar Mayer, and Her Royal Highness, Freeway Kitty, for keeping me company (read being pains in the butt) throughout all the rewrites. Freeway's considerable girth draped across my idle keyboard and Oscar's gentle nudge (dropping his tennis ball at my feet) when I stopped typing for a while, reminded me to get back to work.

Table of Contents

FOREWORD

Soon after patenting his first phonograph to play audio, Thomas Edison mastered the technology to offer owners of the phonograph the ability to record personal messages.

Some twenty years ago, Allen Koenigsberg, a collector of Edison phonographs and recordings, made an extraordinary discovery. In a cache of some three dozen old cylinders, only one of which was anything spectacular, he discovered the recording of a man confessing to a string of killings. The speaker voices his regrets for only one murder... that of his mistress, Minnie Williams.

After some research, Koenigsberg realized that the words on the cylinder were straight out of a confession made by Dr. H. H. Holmes. The only time the recording deviates from the confession is when the man voices regret over his mistress's death. The technology was available, and the equipment was indeed portable enough, that this voice could actually be that of the infamous Holmes. The transcript of the recording follows, and the deviation from Holmes' confession is in bold italics:

"During the past few months, it has been repeatedly expressed that I make a detailed confession of all the graver crimes that have been traced out and brought home to me.

"I have been tried for murder, convicted and sentenced. The first step of my execution, on May 7th [1896], the reading of the death warrant, has been carried out and it now seems a fitting time, if ever, to make known the details of my murders. It would be useless to longer say that I am not guilty in face of the overwhelming amount of proof that has been brought together, not only in one but in each and every case. I will say that the detectives have gone over my entire life and hardly a day or an act has escaped their scrutiny. And ... [false start]

"I am moved to make this confession for a variety of reasons, but among them are not those of bravado, or a desire to parade my wrongdoings, but I do so, as it would be the height of folly to say, without pity. But what is born in the child must come out in the man. I am not sorry, for it would not do any good for me. *I regret only one murder — and that was of Minnie Williams — because I think I loved her. Well, it's done now and I think I made a good job of it.*

"Eighteen months I have passed in solitary confinement and in a few days I am to be led forth to my death. It would now seem a fitting time for me to express regret or remorse, as this I intend to be my last public utterance. But I was born with the Devil in me and I cannot help the fact that I was a murderer, no more than the poet can help the inspiration to a song. I was born with the Evil One standing beside the bed when I was ushered into the world and he has been with me ever since."

Koenigsberg also found a poster used to promote Detective Frank Geyer's book, The Holmes-Pitezel Case. The illustrations included with this foreword are sections from that poster.

Without the records of Moyamensing Prison, which sources report were "scattered to the four winds," it is impossible to ever know for sure if the recently-discovered recording is, indeed, Holmes' voice. The deviation from his confession, from the words "But what is born in the child...," through the words "as this I intend to be my last public utterance...," wording of the text that deviates from his confession, however, strongly suggests that the wax cylinder did, indeed, capture for posterity the tiniest personal scrap of Dr. H. H. Holmes. This writer, as well as Mr. Koenigsburg, believe the recording to be that of Herman Mudgett, alias Dr. H. H. Holmes.

The publishers of Detective Frank Geyer's book, *The Holmes-Pitezel Case*, did not shy away from yellow journalism when promoting their book. The two graphics here are portions of a promotional poster.

(Courtesy Allen Koenigsburg)

"Yes, I was born with the devil in me."

H. H. Holmes

Chapter One

The Birth of a Monster

Winter had begun to loosen its grip on the city of brotherly love when Herman W. Mudgett, alias Dr. H. H. Holmes, put pen to paper in the gloom of Moyamensing Prison and began his final confession. So isolated was he in his cell that the scratch of the pen and his own breathing were the only sounds intruding on his solitude. The nine by fourteen foot room, with its whitewashed walls and concrete floor, had borne witness to many other writings by Holmes. This one, however, would be very different in tone and content from the previous documents.

"Yes, I was born with the devil in me," he wrote. "I could not help the fact that I was a murderer no more than the poet can help the inspiration to song, nor the ambition of an intellectual man to be great. I was born with the evil one standing as my sponsor beside the bed where I was ushered into the world, and he has been with me since. The inclination to murder

Herman Webster Mudgett
(*The Holmes-Pitezel Case*;
**Frank Geyer; Philadelphia:
Publisher's Union, 1896)**

came to me as naturally as the inspiration to do good comes to other men."

But all this came toward the end of Holmes' life. At this point, he had only 25 days of his thirty-six years on earth left to live.

❧

Through a veil of pain and resentment, Theodate Mudgett gave birth to her fourth child and named him Herman Webster. What Theodate could not know was that the tiny infant she held to her breast on May 16, 1860, would become America's most prolific serial killer. Herman took his place beside eight-year-old Ellen, six-year-old Clarence, and two-year-old Arthur.

Since motherhood had failed to soften Theodate before Herman's arrival, his birth could hardly be expected to make a difference. And, indeed, it did not. Her sharp, severe features reflected her cold and distant demeanor. Theodate ruled her family with an iron hand and rigid religion. A school teacher until the time of her marriage, Mother Mudgett paradoxically appeared to harbor no fondness for children, whether her own or someone else's.

Levi's coarse features were a perfect complement to his wife's; the two were American Gothic in the flesh. Levi was a fairly successful

In this house, which still stands, America's most prolific serial killer was born in May of 1860.
(*The Holmes-Pitezel Case*; Frank Geyer;
Philadelphia: Publisher's Union, 1896)

farmer as well as postmaster for Gilmanton Corners. A brutal taskmaster, he never passed up an opportunity to apply the rod. When one of the children sought relief from a toothache, Levi pulled the offending molar or bicuspid himself. Should the child cry out from the agony of Papa's procedure, a cloth reeking of kerosene would be roughly clamped over nose and mouth. Levi's viselike embrace would secure their thrashing limbs until the noxious fumes silenced the children's cries and stilled their bodies. Perhaps Herman's later fondness for using chloroform on his victims sprang from these particular experiences.

Devout Christians, both parents dragged the children to Sunday worship and Wednesday prayer meetings without fail. The Congregationalist Church across the street was their home away from

Gilmanton's Congregationalist Church.
(*The Holmes-Pitezel Case;* **Frank Geyer; Philadelphia: Publisher's Union, 1896)**

home. This was a time when strict, harsh discipline was considered the hallmark of a good parent. Whether he had that fact in mind, or maybe to help his parents save face in light of the grisly charges levied against their son, years later in Moyamensing Prison, Herman would write of his parents,

"That I was well trained by loving and religious parents, I know, and any deviations in my after life from the straight and narrow way of rectitude are not attributable to the want of a tender mother's prayers or a father's control, emphasized, when necessary, by the liberal use of the rod wielded by no sparing hand."

Herman was one of the brightest boys at school, which did nothing for his social life. Frail and unfriendly, Herman was a loner who was often preyed upon by the town bullies.

Every day, Herman had to walk past the home and office of the village physician, Dr. Wight. Because of stories the youngster had heard about the sinister and mysterious goings on there, as well as the strange odors that sometimes wafted forth, Herman was terrified of the place.

He always crossed to the other side of the road and gave Dr. Wight's office a wide berth.

To Herman's great misfortune, some older classmates learned of his abhorrence to the physician's property. As the little boy plodded his way home one day, two of the bullies dragged him, kicking and screaming, inside Dr. Wight's office. They brought him face-to-face with a morbidly grinning skeleton and dumped him at its feet. When Dr. Wight came home later, he found Herman curled around those dangling, clicking toes, catatonic with horror. The boy was only six years old at the time. Horrified as he was, Herman would later credit this episode to his initial interest in a medical career.

When Herman was eight, an itinerant photographer with a pronounced limp came to town and gladly accepted the boy's offer to run errands. In return, the photographer would take Herman's picture for free. The man met Herman at the door one morning, opening it just enough to hand the boy two pieces of a broken wooden rectangle. At the man's bidding, Herman took them to the village wagon maker and instructed him to fashion a new one. The photographer was sitting near the door, partially clothed, when Herman returned with the finished product. The man locked the door and proceeded to remove the greater part of one leg.

"Having never seen or even known that such a thing as artificial limbs existed, my consternation can better be imagined than described," Herman later wrote. "Had he next proceeded to remove his head in the same mysterious way I should not have been further

surprised. He must have noticed my discomfiture, for as soon as his mending process had sufficiently progressed he quickly placed me in a dim light, and standing upon his whole leg, and meantime waving the other at me, he took my picture, which in a few days he gave me. I kept it for many years and the thin terror-stricken face of that bare-footed, home-spun clad boy I can yet see."

This marker stands on the spot where Herman Mudgett's ancestors, the first colonists in the Gilmanton area, settled in 1761 – exactly a century before Herman's birth.

(Snavely Collection)

Gilmanton Corners was as isolated as a community could be in those days. Railroads were booming, but the only proof Gilmanton had of that was an occasional locomotive whistle in the distance. Newspapers were practically unknown. Yet Herman managed to run across one periodical in which he found an advertisement for a gold watch and chain.

Only a few watches could be sold at the ridiculously low price quoted, and the ad urged those desirous of this bargain to act immediately.

Herman rushed to his room and opened the wooden box that contained all his wealth. He dumped the contents onto his bed. Every coin, every penny, had its own particular history for Herman, and he was loath to part with any of them. But he wanted that watch. So he hurried to the village shoemaker and converted the coins into paper currency. He was thrilled -- it was just enough to make the coveted purchase.

Worried that all the watches would be sold before his payment was received, Herman fretted over the mail every day for the next couple of weeks, his stomach in knots. He was jubilant when the timepiece finally arrived. He turned the watch over in his hands, feeling its weight, its cool, smooth metal. He wound it, listening to its measured ticks, and then set it to the correct time. Deciding which pocket to honor with this treasure, Herman went off to find his only close friend, Tom Eschler.

Tom accompanied Herman around town and, at each stop, nonchalantly inquired as to the time of day. Herman proudly pulled the watch from his pocket, flicked it open, and furnished the requested information. In exchange for his supporting role in that little piece of theater, Tom would be allowed to wear the watch for half the day – but only in Herman's presence, lest any harm should befall the prize. Shortly after they embarked on the first part of their plan, the wheels of the watch ceased to turn and the gold began to lose its luster. Rather than a source of pride, the watch became yet another source of ridicule for his tormentors, causing Herman to feel foolish.

Herman embarked upon his life of crime early. At age nine, he swelled the size of the family's cattle herd by "borrowing" a few animals from a neighbor's meadow. As he trotted behind them one morning, prodding them toward the pasture, Herman encountered the man from whom he had purloined the cows.

"Whose be they?" the neighbor, named Richard, asked.

"Ours," Herman replied proudly.

"What, all of them?" asked Richard.

"Yes, *all*, everyone, and that best one is mine, my own," Herman said.

Upon returning home, Herman found Levi waiting for him, demanding to know why the boy had stolen and then lied to Richard (the owner) about the cows. Before Herman could answer, his father produced a familiar leather strop and proceeded to flail the boy within an inch of his life. After the strapping, Herman was banished to his room, ordered to speak to no one, and told he would not be fed for the next two days.

Later that afternoon, staring out his window, he saw Tom perched on the fence, looking lonely and miserable. After much pantomime and gesturing, Tom left and returned with a generous supply of food. Using his ever-present ball of twine, Herman raised the booty up into his room, significantly blunting his punishment for rustling the cattle. Along with the food was a note in Tom's scrawling hand vowing revenge. They would, he suggested, go down and let Richard's cows into his cornfield on the following Saturday, a plan Herman enthusiastically embraced.

Gilmanton Post Office
(*The Holmes-Pitezel Case*; Frank Geyer;
Philadelphia: Publisher's Union, 1896)

Late that night, Herman's mother came and fetched him to her own room. There she knelt down with him and prayed and pled for God to forgive her wayward son. For hours they knelt on the cold, hard floor, knees screaming for relief, until Theodate was satisfied her youngest son had earnestly repented. It was some time before Herman forgot that interlude, and, consequently, the plan for vengeance against his neighbor was never fulfilled.

Tom and Herman's next mischief was perpetrated during their summer break from school. They wrote a rather unpleasant note to an unpopular teacher who, they believed, was to be replaced the following year. In his own words, Herman describes the result:

"I had abundant evidence during the first day of the following term that [the teacher] had received our letter, when he changed my seat from one I had long occupied, and which was very favorably located for looking into the street, to the opposite side of the room. My seatmate was a very disagreeable and unpopular girl."

One summer the two boys agreed to pull a farmer's weeds for what Herman called "a ridiculously small pittance." The weeds were strong and as tall as the boys, but they toiled under the hot sun until every green thing in the field had been uprooted. When, weary and hungry, they held out small, blistered hands for their pay, it was not forthcoming. Though they returned several times to ask for their money, the farmer never came through. Convinced that further pleading was useless, Tom and Herman returned to the field and, soon, the seeds from all the weeds they had pulled had been broadcast across the now-bare soil.

Herman would later write of this incident,

"...it so well illustrates the principle that many times in my after life influenced me to make my conscience become blind."

One of the most significant events of Herman's childhood years took place when he was eleven years old. The old Gant place just outside of town was rumored to be haunted, the result of its owner's macabre death. According to legend, Gant was said to have been dead long before his bones were found, stripped of meat by his ravenous dogs. Gant had always been considered strange, and now the house was thought to be as strange as its previous tenant.

Intrigued, Tom and Herman walked to Gant's place and warily approached. They crept into the house, giggling and making great sport of trying to spook one another. Somehow, while the two were cavorting on the second floor, Tom fell down the stairs. The fall broke the boy's neck and he was dead when his body came to rest on the first-floor landing. Herman never made another close friend, nor did it seem that he missed having one. In hindsight, it's valid to wonder if Tom wasn't Herman's first homicide victim.

Shortly after Tom's death, Herman began conducting "experiments" on small animals. At first he simply dissected whatever creatures he found already dead. Then he graduated to live animals. Over the next couple of years, he became more and more proficient at keeping the unfortunate beasts alive for longer periods of time while he sliced them open to see how everything inside worked.

When his bloodlust could no longer be sated with those smaller creatures, Herman set his sights on larger prey.

> "I could hardly count my Western trip a
> failure, however, for I had seen Chicago."
>
> *Dr. H. H. Holmes*

Chapter Two

Dr. Holmes, I Presume

A web of lies, half-truths, and deceit, Holmes' memoirs devotes less than one paragraph to his life between ages sixteen and nineteen. His first, and only legitimate, marriage and the birth of his son Robert are not mentioned in those scant few lines.

After graduating the academy, Herman taught in the local elementary school. The rapacious beast that now controlled his every action demanded greater acts of sadism to attain sexual gratification. Herman's torture of small animals

This sketch was made in Ann Arbor, MI, for the University of Michigan Medical School's class of 1884.

12

**The city's offices now occupy Gilmanton Academy.
(Snavely Collection)**

escalated rapidly, each subsequent deed more heinous than its prede-
cessor. Soon, the slaughter and dissection of four-legged creatures no
longer satisfied his needs and Herman turned his sights on human prey.
In order to make the most of his human conquests, he decided to attain
a medical degree. Stifled by the lack of funds for such an education, he
watched helplessly as the seasons passed, desperate to break free of his
home town's constrictions.

As he proved so often throughout his short life, Herman let nothing
come between him and his desires. So, at the age of eighteen, he eloped
with Clara A. Lovering and was married before a justice of the peace in
Alton, New Hampshire. Herman's main motive for marrying Clara was
to get his hands on her recently-acquired inheritance. Within a year of

their marriage, he set off for the University of Michigan Medical School in Ann Arbor, financed by his pliable and now-pregnant wife.

"After having paid my college fees, bought my books and other articles necessary for my second year in college, I found myself hundreds of miles away from friends and relatives, and with about $60 in money with nine months of hard study before me..."

Though Clara's money covered the basics, it was hardly enough to provide the lifestyle that Herman craved. His voracious appetite for the finer things in life demanded immediate gratification, and so, at this point, he began to perfect a scheme upon which he would fall back numerous times throughout his life.

Herman would take out phony life insurance policies and then cash them in by producing the dead body of the "insured." Some of the bodies were "borrowed" from the anatomy lab of the medical school; some were taken from nearby morgues and funeral parlors. He was actually caught in the act of snatching a corpse from the anatomy lab and somehow talked his way out of expulsion. Some of his earliest homicides were most likely committed during this period, as well. That he worked the insurance scheme throughout his medical training is certain. How many *lives* he may have claimed in the process will never be known. That knowledge died with him on the gallows at Moyamensing Prison.

In the quiet of late night, his presence obscured by darkness, Herman raided local graveyards. In his memoirs he flatly denies these actions.

"The limits of this book will not allow me to write the many quaint and some ghastly experiences of our medical education were

I otherwise disposed to do so. Suffice it to say that they stopped far
short of desecration of country graveyards, as has been repeatedly
charged, as it is a well-known fact that in the State of Michigan all
the material necessary for dissection work is legitimately supplied
by the State."

Herman emphasizes as a "well-known fact" that the school's dissecting needs were fully met by the state. Only in Herman's own mind
was The University of Michigan Medical School ever included in the
body-snatching accusations aimed his way. A gifted liar, he wove together fact and fiction so convincingly that, in time, even *he* embraced
his version of the truth as fact.

He spent a grueling summer following his junior year as a sales
representative for a Chicago book agent and, previous cattle rustling
notwithstanding, said "...in this venture I committed the first really
dishonest act of my life." Apparently, cattle rustling did not fall within
the guidelines of Herman's definition of "dishonest." To justify his
actions and sway public sentiment, Herman calls the book as well as
the firm a "fraud," saying he was promised hundreds of dollars in com-
missions. He states,

"...after the most strenuous efforts, having succeeding [sic] in
selling a sufficient number to defray my expenses and pay my return
fare to Ann Arbor, I came back without making a settlement with
the firm there, and for the remainder of my vacation earned what
money I could in and about the college city."

Herman Webster Mudgett, alias Dr. H. H. Holmes.
(*The Holmes-Pitezel Case; Frank Geyer*; Philadelphia: Publisher's Union, 1896)

His final comment on this venture, darkly menacing in retrospect, was, "I could hardly count my Western trip a failure, however, for I had seen Chicago."

In June of 1884, Herman left Ann Arbor, a newly-minted medical doctor. A dispatch from the university following his arrest many years later confirmed he was, indeed, a member of the class of '84.

Herman briefly returned to the bosom of his family in Gilmanton following graduation. Wife Clara had given birth to a healthy son, Robert Lovering Mudgett, and the toddler became the subject of his father's first human dissecting experiment. Though he stopped short of killing the boy, Herman permanently disfigured Robert. In his final confession, he does not go into much detail about what he did to Robert, nor did Herman mention how he explained this malicious deed to Clara.

Herman shook the dust of New Hampshire off his shoes and headed out to make his fortune. In his westward journey, the new doctor held a rapid succession of unsuccessful jobs in several different cities. He nearly starved that winter practicing medicine and teaching school in Mooers Forks, New York.

"During my long years [actually only two years] there in New York I had abundant time to work out the details of a scheme that my University friend [a Canadian student] and myself had talked over during our hungry college days as a possible last resort in case our medical practice proved a failure; and from certain letters I had received from him, I judged that he, too, had not found all his hardships at an end upon receiving his diploma. I therefore went to where he was located, and found that though his experience had been less disheartening than my own, it had from a pecuniary standpoint been far from successful."

Though Mudgett claims at this point he and his friend "perfected" their insurance scheme, what actually happened was the death of his friend while in Herman's company. Following graduation, that particular student drowned while the two were out rowing. Mudgett penned this convoluted explanation:

"At some future date a man whom my friend knew and could trust, who then carried considerable life insurance, was to increase the same so that the total amount carried should be $40,000; and as he was a man of moderate circumstances he was to have it understood that some sudden danger he had escaped (a runaway accident) had impelled him to more fully protect his family in the future. Later he should become addicted to drink, and while tem-

porarily insane from its use should, as it would appear afterwards, kill his wife and child.

"In reality they were to go to the extreme West and await his arrival there at a later date. Suddenly the husband was to disappear, and some months later a body badly decomposed and dressed in the clothing he was known to wear was to be found, and with it a statement to the effect that while in a drunken rage he had killed his family and had shipped their dismembered bodies to two separate and distant warehouses to conceal the crime, first having partially preserved the remains by placing them in strong brine. That he did not care to live longer, and that his property and insurance should pass to a relative whom he was to designate in this letter.

"At the proper time he was to join his family in the West, and remain there permanently, the relative collecting the insurance, a part of which was to be sent to him, a part to be retained by the relative, and the remainder to be divided between us.

This scheme called for a considerable amount of material, no less than three bodies in fact. This difficulty was easily overcome, however, so long as it was supposed that they were needed for experimental purposes, but no doctor could call for three bodies at one time without exciting suspicion, and so it was arranged that I was to go to Chicago for the winter, and sometime during the intervening months we should both contribute toward the necessary supply."

Before he arrived in Chicago, however, Herman spent time working as a clerk in a Minneapolis drug store, where he met Myrta Belknap, who would play a prominent role in his life in the following years.

He ventured on to Philadelphia and spent a brief stint at the Norristown Asylum. Of his work at the asylum, Herman says that "this was my first experience with insane persons, and so terrible was it that for years afterwards, even now sometimes, I see their faces in my sleep. Fortunately within a few days after entering the Asylum I received word that I could obtain different employment in a drug store on Columbia Avenue, which I at once accepted."

Though his Canadian friend is now dead he continues to color him as a viable entity in his complicated scheme.

"Meantime, my friend had promptly obtained his portion [of human remains] and placed it in the storage in Delaware from which place it was shipped to me later in Chicago. I remained in Minneapolis until May, 1886, when I returned to Chicago...I had prior to this made arrangements to furnish my portion of the material. After reaching Chicago, certain sudden changes in my plans called me hastily to New York City, and I decided to take a part of the material there and leave the balance in a Chicago warehouse. This necessitated the repacking of the same, and to accomplish this I went to a hotel (May, 1886), where I registered under an assumed name, and occupied a room and had the package, which had been shipped from Detroit, taken there, and carefully removing the car-

pet from one portion of the room I divided the material into two packages. In doing this the floor became discolored.

"Later, one of these packages was placed in the Fidelity Storage Warehouse in Chicago, and the other I took with me to New York and placed it in a safe place. Upon my trip from Chicago to New York I read two accounts of the detection of crime connected with this class of work, and for the first time I realized how well organized and well prepared the leading insurance companies were to detect and punish this kind of fraud, and this, together with a letter I received upon reaching my destination, and the sudden death of my friend, caused all to be abandoned."

Herman concocted this entire bizarre story to explain away the physical evidence gathered from the various lodgings he had occupied since graduation from medical school. In his own mind, the killer dehumanized his victims by referring to the corpses as "material."

Herman was forced to depart his Philadelphia drug store job in a rush. All versions of the story, with the single exception of his own, say he fled after a female customer was poisoned by medicine he prepared the very morning of the day he left town. His memoirs read,

"About July 1ˢᵗ, one afternoon, a child entered the store and exclaimed, 'I want a doctor! The medicine we got here this morning has killed my brother (or sister).' I could remember no sale that morning corresponding to the one she hastily described, but I made sure that a physician was at once sent to the house, and having done this I hastily wrote a note to my employer stating the nature of the

trouble, and left the city immediately for Chicago, and it was not until nine years later that I knew the result of the case."

To dodge the charges against him in Philadelphia, Herman fled to Chicago, arriving in the summer of 1886. From the moment he stepped off the train on the depot's landing, Herman Webster Mudgett ceased to exist. In his place was Dr. Henry H. Holmes, and the career of America's most prolific serial killer began in earnest.

"The inclination to murder came to me as naturally as the inspiration to do right comes to the majority of persons."

H. H. Holmes

Chapter Three

That Toddlin' Town

Finding that he could not work as a pharmacist until passing an examination, Herman headed to Springfield, Illinois for that purpose. He registered as Dr. Henry Howard Holmes, the nom de plume by which he would become infamous, and used that name for the majority of his killing career. After securing his certification as a druggist, Dr. Holmes returned to Chicago.

In 1886, the suburb of Englewood was a well-to-do area just south of Chicago's city limits. Today, it is considered one of the *worst* sections of the city. But a hundred and twenty years ago, it was quite the tony place to live. The Chamber of Commerce boasted that Englewood was "the best locality for suburban residence in the vicinity of Chicago... seven leading lines of railway furnish 45 trains each way daily. All of these trains must stop at Englewood."

Less than a block from the train station, at 63rd and Wallace, stood Dr. E. S. Holton's drug store. On the hot day in July when Holmes wandered inside the modest shop, its owner was terminally ill with prostate cancer. Mrs. Holton was trying to hold the business together, and was grateful to turn the business over to the dapper young man who offered his services that day.

Holmes was a relatively small man, 5' 7" tall and 150 pounds, but he had an erect, manly carriage and was quite attractive. He was never seen in public without a bowler hat perched atop his dark brown hair, and his slate-blue eyes sparkled with intelligence. He sported a handlebar mustache, which curled gently at the ends above his full lower lip.

Holmes was an immediate hit with the ladies. As he guided them through the myriad colored jars and sparkling bottles, he flirted outrageously with them all and delighted in their admiration. As the summer wore on, Dr. Holton became weaker and weaker, Mrs. Holton less and less involved in the store's affairs, and by August, Holmes was handling every aspect of the store's operations. He was clerk, druggist, and bookkeeper, and Mrs. Holton was more than happy to let him take

498   TOWN OF LAKE BUSINESS DIRECTORY.

DRESSMAKERS—CONTINUED.

Preston Sadie I. es State 2d s 61st, Englewood
Putnam Lottie Miss, 635 Gordon
Rhoades B. C. Mrs. 5564 Atlantic, Englewood
Scott Cora A. Miss, es Winter 1st s 68th, Normal Park
Steel Wiliam Mrs. 548 Duncan Park
Sterrit Maggie Miss, 716, 47th
Stoller Minnie Miss, 4351 Butterfield
Stowe M. Mrs. 6242 Wentworth av, Englewood
STRICKLAND JULIA MRS. 426, 61st
Sweetman Maggie Miss, 4161 Wentworth av
Toliaferro Mrs. T. T. ns of 65th 1st e Halsted, Englewood
Troy J. C. Mrs. 4829 Justine
Wade Phœbe C. Mrs. 755 Gordon
Walker E. Mrs. 423. 59th, Englewood
WENNERSKOLD C. A. MRS. 5238 Wentworth
  av (see adv p. III)
Yerty M. D. Miss, 6435 Wentworth av

DRUGGISTS.

BARNES JOHN, 825, 43d
Bell John I. 4700 State
BONHEIM FRANK, 4358 State
BONHEIM LEE M. 5421 Wentworth av
CALDWELL PETER, 711, 43d
CORY V. P & CO. 4101 State
DIETZ JOHN, 3905 Wentworth av
HOGAN & HISGEN, 6214 Wentworth av, Englewood
HOLTON E. S. 63d cor Wallace, Englewood
HOUGHTON H. J. 6560 Wentworth av, Englewood
HURST N. N. 5100 Wentworth av and 3906 State
HURST'S PHARMACIES, 5100 Wentworth av and
  3906 State
Justi W. F. 4644 Wentworth av
KOTZENBERG CHARLES, 4203 S. Halsted
Masquelet John, 47th cor Bishop
Mehl William, 4658 Ashland av
NORTH CHARLES F. Tillotson Block, Englewood
PIERPOINT BROS. ws Lincoln av 2d n of 68th,
  Englewood
PORTER M. N. & CO. State cor 39th and Indiana
  av cor 39th
REASNER & CO. 5727 Wentworth av, Englewood
Ritter A. Paul, 4341 Halsted
Sandmeyer Henry, 736, 43d

The 1886 Englewood Directory listed Holton's
Drug Store at 63rd & Wallace.
(Courtesy of the Abraham Lincoln Presidential Library)

**Holton's Drug Store stood on the right corner of
this ALDI Discount Store's parking lot.
(Snavely Collection)**

over her affairs.

Shortly after Dr. Holton's death in August, Holmes took advantage of the widow's grief and approached her about buying the drug store. Holmes' offer seemed the ideal situation for the widow, allowing her to stay in the little apartment above the store. Dr. Holton had been her only family, and with him gone she wished to live out her days where she and her husband had carved their life together.

The young doctor became a familiar figure in the neighborhood, commuting between his suburban lodgings and work. Nobody knew exactly where Holmes lived and when asked, he was elusive. With walking stick in hand and bowler perched jauntily atop his head, Holmes strolled the neighborhood, impressing the men and charming the ladies. His fellow merchants considered him well spoken and industrious – an asset to the community.

The grieving Mrs. Holton, however, was quickly becoming disillusioned. Though he had agreed to pay $100 monthly on his purchase, Holmes was not keeping his end of the bargain. He was evasive when asked about the payments and began to avoid the widow, no mean feat with her living above his store. Relations between the two became rancorous and bitter, and Mrs. Holton threatened legal action. When the threat itself failed, she retained counsel and filed suit against her former savior. Holmes' version of this situation is, of course, quite different:

"A little later I bought [the drugstore], paying for it for the most part with money secured by mortgaging the stock and fixtures, agreeing to repay this loan at the rate of $100 per month. My trade was good, and for the first time in my life I was established in a business that was satisfactory to me.

"But very soon my landlord, seeing that I was prospering well, made me aware that my rent would be increased and to protect myself I was forced to purchase at a great expense the vacant property opposite the location I then occupied, and to erect a building thereon."

Shortly after Mrs. Holton filed suit, she suddenly and mysteriously disappeared. Holmes broadcast the story that the lady had moved to be with relatives in California, the memories in the small apartment she shared with her husband too painful to bear. Holmes gave up his rented rooms and moved into the little apartment just "vacated" by Dr. Holton's widow. The lady was never seen or heard from again.

The eligible young ladies in the neighborhood, as well as their mothers, were supremely disappointed when Dr. Holmes suddenly brought home a bride from out of state. He married Myrta Belknap, the young woman from Minneapolis, on January 28, 1887. His conscience a little prickly over this action, he filed for divorce from his legal wife, Clara, a few weeks later...romantically enough, on Valentine's Day. But the suit was dismissed "for default of appearance of complainant." Still, his affection for Myrta must have been genuine, for Holmes, however briefly, considered doing the honorable thing – the only documented proof of him ever doing right in his life.

The newlyweds set up house in the little apartment above the drug store, and Myrta worked contentedly beside her husband for several months. Quiet and contemplative, Myrta's personality was a sharp contrast to Holmes' outgoing charm, but it was obvious the new Mrs. Holmes adored her husband.

Myrta fled with baby Lucy to her parents' house in Wilmette, IL.

(*The Chicago Times;* August, 1896; Courtesy of the Abraham Lincoln Presidential Library)

At first, Holmes made some effort to curtail his outrageous flirting to spare his bride's feelings. But eventually, even Myrta's presence failed to hamper his blatant womanizing, and she was seen in the store less frequently. Holmes loved the ladies, and not even the affection he held for Myrta could modify his behavior for long. Myrta was trying to make the best of her situation and endeavored to be unconcerned about her husband's behavior, preferring to see his actions as gallantry. Pained by Holmes' flirtations, she began to make mild protests which elicited sharp retorts from her husband. Tension mounted between the two, and Myrta's protests became angry accusations.

During the next year, patrons began to witness increasingly embarrassing scenes, generally ending with Holmes hissing sharp barbs and Myrta storming upstairs in tears. The situation soon became intolerable, but divorce was out of the question. On Holmes' part, filing for divorce might bring some facts to light that he preferred to leave buried. Myrta loved her husband despite his faults and deplored the stigma of divorce. In any case, by the spring of 1888, she was pregnant and divorce was no longer an option.

At the nucleus of Englewood's burgeoning economy and located in such close proximity to the bustling train station, Holmes and his drug store were thriving. But his wife was not. The noise and constant activity swirling around her began to take its toll on Myrta.

When her parents moved to nearby Wilmette, Holmes'

Myrta and Lucy Holmes.

(*The Philadelphia Inquirer;* July, 1895; Courtesy of the Free Library of Philadelphia.)

pregnant wife moved in with them to avoid being a daily witness to her husband's constant philandering. He agreed to provide financial support and pay regular visits. Customers who inquired about Myrta's whereabouts were told that her delicate condition, as well as the din of the nearby train station, had put her in a state of nervous exhaustion. Though he longed to have her by his side, Holmes told customers, with the store demanding so much of his time, he thought it best to place Myrta in the loving hands of her parents in Wilmette.

But truth be known, living alone on Sixty-third Street was essential for Holmes to satisfy his malevolent desires. Customers continued to look upon their local druggist as a paragon, and Holmes played the role brilliantly. He hungrily consumed the how-to and motivational literature of the time, such as Andrew Carnegie's *The Road to Business Success.*

Holmes' Daughter, Lucy (*The Philadelphia Inquirer;* July, 1895; Courtesy of the Free Library of Philadelphia.)

Holmes nurtured a dark vision of colossal proportions; one so ambitious that the little corner drug store could serve only as the venue to oversee its realization. And so, in the summer of 1888, he secured a lease on the vacant property across from his store and began plans to erect a magnificent building. Shortly after Myrta moved out, he began to draw the blueprints for what would become known worldwide as Holmes' Castle.

Given the ethics of the Gilded Age, Holmes' lust for wealth and his grandiose vision were admired. However, passersby could never have fathomed the malicious intent of his creation.

"Where others' hearts were touched with pity, mine filled with cruelty, and where in others the feeling was to save life, I reveled [sic] in the thought of destroying same."

H. H. Holmes

Chapter Four

Holmes Castle

In the fall of 1888, construction began on the building that the *Chicago Times* would later describe as a "murder factory." The place

Pat Quinlan.
(*Chicago Times-Herald*, July 25, 1895;
Courtesy Abraham Lincoln
Presidential Library).

was only three stories tall with a full basement, but it sprawled across every inch of the fifty by a hundred and sixty-two foot lot. Amidst the percussion of hammers, the whine of saws, and the pungent smell of sawdust, something more than an ordinary hotel was being erected.

Holmes hired Pat Quinlan, a sinister-looking thug, and introduced him as his new janitor. In fact, Quinlan had been retained to add

Sketch of Holmes Castle
(*United Press International;* Courtesy Abraham
Lincoln Presidential Library).

features to the structure that had previously only been found in horror novels. Each floor contained 8,000 square feet of space, and at the very core of the building, Quinlan worked on the amenities necessary to convert Holmes' darkest fantasies into reality.

Neighbors milled about the bustling site, marveling at the scope of Holmes' dream. What they probably failed to notice was how quickly the faces of the work crews changed. As soon as a crew requested payment, Holmes would fire them on the spot, claiming shoddy workmanship. He didn't mind that this practice slowed completion, for his manner of handling crews was extremely economical. In addition to saving money, keeping fresh faces on the site avoided any one laborer from ever getting a clear idea of what exactly was being built. Holmes could ill afford to arouse curiosity about his unorthodox floor plans.

A clutch of airtight rooms lined from floor to ceiling with asbestos-covered steel plates were located in the heart of the Castle. Some were also soundproofed, and many had been plumbed with gas pipes whose controls were located in Holmes' bedroom. Some rooms were little more than narrow closets with low ceilings. One room had been divided horizontally into two levels with a trap door connecting the two levels. There were peepholes, secret passageways, closets hidden behind sliding panels, trapdoors to nowhere, and greased chutes to the basement for easy disposal of pesky corpses.

At some point during construction, the building was christened with the lofty title of Castle, and once uttered, the term caught on and the building was referred to thereafter as Holmes' Castle. When the Castle was finished, more than 500 workers had contributed to its completion. Using traditional and orthodox labor practices, the place could have been completed in a third of the time.

Holmes treated his suppliers no better than his work crews. He ordered everything he needed on credit, supplies and materials that soon became part of the Castle's infrastructure, and never paid for them. When the more ambitious creditors brought suit against him, Holmes managed to keep the cases tied up in court. Few who provided goods and services toward completion of Holmes' Castle ever collected payment.

It was during the construction of the Castle that Holmes acquired the services of Benjamin F. Pitezel, who soon became his constant companion. With Pitezel's ominous presence, *physical* threats from disgruntled creditors against the good doctor also came to naught. Of Pitezel, who obviously had a very creative mind, Holmes wrote in his memoirs:

> *"Coming to him at his work I would find him with a set of figures and perhaps a diagram illustrative of their use, or busy making a model of some complicated contrivance. This proceeded so far that for my own protection I had to cause him to work by contract instead of by the day, although I found him fully as im-provident of his own time as he had been of mine."*

Benjamin Pitezel.
**(*The Holmes-Pitezel Case;*
Frank Geyer; Philadelphia:
Publisher's Union, 1896)**

Putting their creative ideas and devious minds together, Holmes and Pitezel planned elaborate secret passages and trap doors throughout the Castle. The truth of what was being constructed at the core of the three-story building was a sacred confidence that Pitezel and Quinlan never violated. It would be several years before those secrets would be exposed.

Blessed with an overabundance of audacity, Holmes ordered a walk-in vault, and when it was delivered, had it lugged to a framed-in room on the Castle's third floor. He ordered the room quickly finished, leaving a doorway far too small for the safe to fit through. Any efforts by the manufacturer to repossess the vault were thwarted because removing it from that room would incur serious damage to the Castle – damage for which the repossessor would be liable. The safe stayed where it was. Holmes had Quinlan run a gas line into the vault and obscured the pipe's presence by hiding it behind supplies.

Holmes contacted Warner Glass Bending Company to have a huge

Holmes' private laboratory in the Castle basement. (*Chicago Times-Herald*; July 25, 1895; Courtesy Abraham Lincoln Presidential Library).

"glass-bending" oven installed in the Castle basement. As Warner finished his work, Holmes lured the inventor into the yawning kiln to explain a few of the finer points of its operation. When Holmes stepped out of the enormous oven, ostensibly to get some tools, he slammed and latched the heavy cast-iron door and turned the gas on full force. Though inquiries were made into the man's disappearance, nobody could have guessed Warner's gruesome fate, and certainly the still very respectable Dr. Holmes was never suspected.

The Castle's first floor was quite ordinary, consisting of shops that faced Sixty-third or Wallace Street. Here Holmes kept his personal office space, along with the walk-in vault, and thirty-six ordinary hotel rooms. It was the upper floors and the basement that embodied the true evil hidden behind the lovely façade of the Holmes' Castle.

On the second-floor, fifty-two doors opened to reveal thirty-five rooms along meandering, bizarrely-angled corridors. Some of the rooms were ordinary hotel rooms. Holmes' own living quarters were on this floor, his windows offering a view of Sixty-third street.

The entry to one of the second-floor rooms was the starting point of a maze which, when successfully traversed, ended in a bathroom with a trapdoor in the floor. The trapdoor revealed a secret stairway to the basement. Adjacent to that stairway was a dummy elevator shaft that led from the third floor to the basement. The elevator car itself sat abandoned in one of the second-floor halls.

Why was the elevator installed in the first place if not to be operational? Why turn an everyday occurrence like a trip to the bathroom into a quest to solve a maze? Many questions offered up by the Holmes Castle can never, will never, be answered. Some of the rooms had extremely low ceilings and trapdoors with ladders that led to smaller rooms beneath. Many of these rooms were only accessible through sliding panels or trap doors.

One reporter speculated that the elevator shaft was just another huge gas chamber. His theory stated that Holmes would render a victim unconscious with the use of chloroform, and then drop them into the shaft

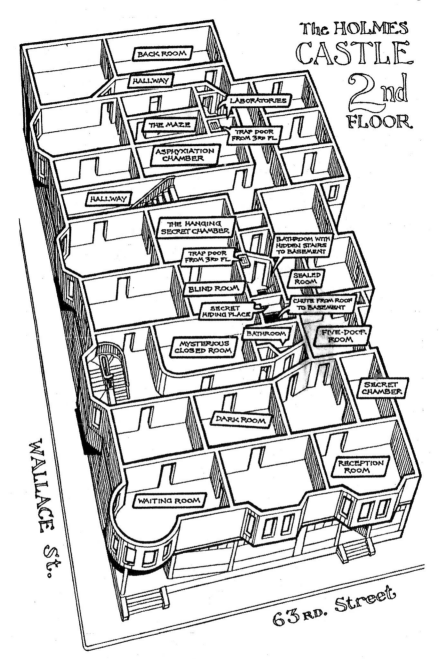

Floor plan of Castle's second floor.
(Courtesy of Rick Geary, author and illustrator of *The Beast of Chicago* graphic novel; www.rickgeary.com)

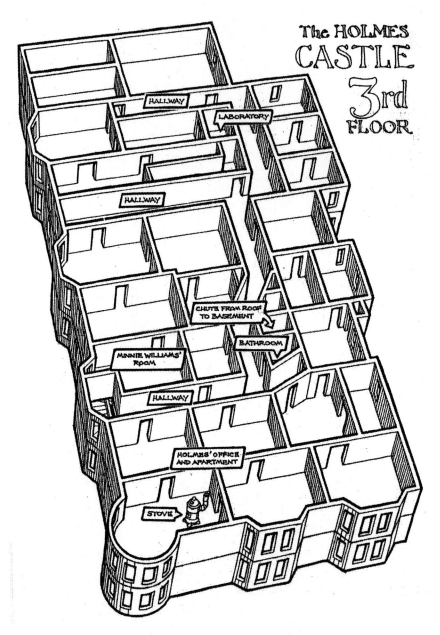

Floor plan of Castle's third floor.
(Courtesy of Rick Geary, author and illustrator of *The Beast of Chicago graphic novel;* www.rickgeary.com)

from the second floor. Trudging up to the third floor, he would open the elevator doors and slide a mammoth, thick sheet of glass over the open shaft, turn on the gas, and watch his victim's panic upon awakening.

Through this false vault door adjacent to his office, Holmes could eavesdrop and watch the people in his office.

(*Philadelphia Inquirer;* April 12, 1896; Courtesy of the Free Library of Philadelphia).

This explanation was probably right on target. A sexual sadist, Holmes would have been wildly aroused by his victims' terror, which would lead to a much more intense release than by simply bedding them.

Since Holmes would do the bulk of his killing on the upper floors, a greased chute provided easy transfer of corpses to the basement. In

Holmes' chambers were the controls to the gas pipes fitted into the airtight rooms and the walk-in vault. Holmes also installed an electric bell in his room which rang when any door was opened on that floor. Every door on the upper stories could be locked only from the outside, and Holmes alone had the keys.

The huge stove in Holmes' office. Human hair, bones, scraps of fabric, and buttons were recovered during the search of the Castle. (*Chicago Times-Herald;* **July 25, 1895; Courtesy Abraham Lincoln Presidential Library).**

The basement, however, was the stuff of which nightmares are made. In that dark, dank dungeon squatted large acid-filled vats and huge, ghostly-white quicklime pits. The enormous Warner furnace sported a grate large enough to accommodate a human body. This grate was also fitted with wheels, rendering the apparatus a perfect crematory. Next to a cabinet filled with Holmes' surgical tools was a dissecting table. One small area, which resembled nothing so much as a medieval torture chamber, was cluttered with bizarre devices. Among these was Dr. Holmes' "elasticity determinator." It was quite simply a torture rack, but Holmes believed it could be used to create a new race of eight-foot-tall giants.

Construction on the Castle was completed in June of 1890. Busy with his new enterprise, Holmes put Horton's old drug store up for sale. It soon caught the interest of a young man from Michigan, A. L. Jones. Newly married, Jones brought his wife to tour the drug store at Holmes' invitation. Prior to the couple's arrival, Holmes assured a favorable impression by hiring people to come in and act as customers while the Joneses were there. The two finally agreed on a price, which just happened to be every dime Jones had to his name. But Holmes' drug store was such a great investment, Jones was sure his money would soon be doubled – even tripled. The store officially changed hands in July of that year.

Shortly after Jones took over his new business, a huge delivery truck showed up in front of the hexagonal entranceway to the Castle's elegant corner store. Into the new structure were carted graceful brass and copper store fixtures, glass-fronted display cabinets, elegant wood cases, and marble counters. A spiked design called a Catherine wheel, so named because it symbolized the instrument of torture involved in the martyrdom of St. Catherine of Alexandria, sprouted at the ceiling over a central Corinthian pillar. Was this an unconscious choice on Holmes' part, or a subtle clue to his eventual purpose?

The marvelous machine that Holmes claimed would turn water into gas. (*Philadelphia Inquirer;* April 12, 1896; Courtesy of the Free Library of Philadelphia).

Elegant watercolor fresco adorned the stucco walls and ceiling over a black and white checkered tile floor. The soda fountain's copper and brass hardware sparkled in the sunlight, and jewel-colored potions glittered on the gleaming walnut shelves of the store proper.

Jones had naturally assumed that his would be the only drug store on the corner of 63rd and Wallace. Jones' reaction to what was going on across the street must have been one of dismay and betrayal. Holmes had promised him he would be unchallenged in that location. The old drug store was gloomy and depressing by comparison to the new one, and Jones was soon forced to close up shop and return to Michigan, a ruined man. What Jones could not know at the time was that he was lucky to have lost only his *money* to Dr. Holmes.

Across the street at the Castle, business was booming, yet Holmes never seemed to have enough money. He had the rents from his tenants and the income from his drug store, but this was the Gilded Age and excess was the god of choice. Millions were being made every day, and Holmes wanted his share. He opened all sorts of businesses on the first floor of the Castle – jewelry stores, restaurants, barbershops, a confectionary. He manufactured soap and bought the ABC Copier Company, which manufactured an ancestor of the mimeograph machine. He swindled, conned, defrauded, and stole, concealing his dishonesty beneath a suave and charming exterior. He was bright, ambitious, energetic – and lethal.

Holmes' mind never rested, and one day he announced that he had bought the rights to a revolutionary machine that could convert ordinary tap water into illuminating gas. He led a group of Canadian investors down into the shadows of his basement where he unveiled his "Chemical-Water Gas Generator." Spouting Medusa-like pipes that angled in all directions, the miracle machine resembled nothing so much as a large front-loading washing machine.

With a flourish, Holmes poured a cupful of water into the machine then meticulously measured the many secret chemicals required and tossed them in, as well. He adjusted a couple of valves, spun some knobs, and gas spewed out the vent. Holmes lit a match and, milking all the drama he could from that action, applied the flame to the stream of gas. *Voila*, it lit. He gleefully watched the investors' expressions as they gaped in wonderment.

The men happily paid Holmes $10,000 for the patent. When Chicago Gas Company heard about Holmes' amazing device, they sent an inspector to take a look. Though difficult to see in the dim light, the inspector succeeded in finding a small pipe that snaked from the back of Holmes' contraption, through the floor of the Castle, and directly into the city gas supply. A testament to Holmes' glib tongue and charming demeanor, the gas company declined to file charges against him. They did, however, confiscate his marvelous machine, leaving an ugly wound in the basement floor. Holmes then erected a brick wall, sealing off the area of the cellar where the machine had stood.

Holmes gave his account this way:

"I think it was in 1889 that I was one day waited upon by two gentlemen who wished to sell me a gas machine, by using which I could be forever independent of the regular city gas company. So great were the inducements held out that I later met them at their

office in La Salle street, and before leaving them had bought one of the machines, which a few days later was arranged in the basement of my building, and I had notified the city company that thereafter I should cease to be one of their patrons. For two days the new machine performed wonders, and I recommended it to many of my customers and friends. The third evening when I was very busy my store was suddenly enveloped in darkness. I was obliged to turn away my customers and close for the want of light, and from then until morning I wrestled with my gas machine; and when Pitezel came to his day's work he found me still perspiring and, I fear, swearing over it...

"That afternoon I instructed him [Pitezel] to temporarily connect it with the city gas to provide light for the evening, and the next day I would go to the company and make a new application to again become a permanent customer. As he finished making the connection he remarked that he thought that it would be a good permanent arrangement without going to the gas company. His quiet remark resulted in my having him, next day, lead the gas from the city main to the machine underground in such a way that it would not be known without a close inspection, and this I did, not to defraud the city, but "to get even" with the company who had defrauded me. A few evenings thereafter the president of this [gas machine] company called upon me, and, after quietly studying my new light for a time, spoke to me of it...

"Several other visits followed, and although I was apparently averse to disposing of my new discovery, I finally did so, taking in return first a contract so skillfully worded that there would later be

no claims brought against me, and, second, a check for a large sum of money. Had matters stopped here as I had at first intended, all would have been well, but I neglected disconnecting from the city supply from day to day, until finally an inspector, more energetic than his fellow-workers, became aware of it, and this resulted in my very willingly choosing to pay a five hundred dollar gas bill in preference to being openly written up and perhaps prosecuted."

Soon after, the H. H. Holmes Pharmacy introduced a new product, Linden Grove Mineral Water. Holmes regaled his customers with praises about the product, supposedly extracted from an artesian well discovered in the basement of the Castle. He sold the water for five cents a glass or twenty-five cents a bottle. The elixir became very popular with neighborhood folks who never knew they were paying a premium for plain tap water laced with vanilla and bitters.

Even with all the money coming in, it was never enough to support the free-wheeling lifestyle Holmes was determined to enjoy. New schemes, fresh cons, and clever scams simmered in the back of his mind. He would employ every one of them before justice finally caught up with him. But that day was still cloaked in the mists of the distant future.

Until then, Holmes had places to go and people to kill.

"I reveled in [torture] with the enthusiasm of an alchemist on the trail of the philosopher's stone."

H. H. Holmes

Chapter Five

The Women of the Castle

The jobs of typewriter and cashier at the Holmes Castle were, quite literally, dead-end jobs. Over the years in Englewood, Holmes went through more female employees than handkerchiefs. The neighborhood buzzed with gossip about the doctor's fondness for women, one nearby business owner estimating the number who entered his employ at over one hundred. Holmes courted them, seduced them, weaseled every dime he could from them, and when he became bored, desecrated their bodies.

"We do know that he understood poisons and their use; that the use of corrosive chemicals was a favorite theme in his conversations with the jeweler Davis; and that disintegration of the tissues of a human being through chemical actions was another of his favorite topics," states David Franke in his book, *The Torture Doctor,* published in 1975.

Another local druggist by the last name of Erickson had serious questions about the good doctor. "Well, he always wanted so much chloroform. During the time I was there, it was only a few months, I sometimes sold him the drug nine or ten times a week and each time it was in large quantities. I asked him what he used it for on several occasions, but he gave me very unsatisfactory answers," the man stated. "At last I refused to let him have any more unless he told me...He then told me that he was making some experiments and the following day showed me a bottle containing yellow fluid. He had another bottle with a white liquid in it, and when he mixed the two, a heavy vapor arose to which he set fire. He also told me that the gas was poisonous. Sometime after that, when he got more chloroform, I asked him if his experiments were nearly complete and then he said that he was not making any experiments. I could never make him out."

The looming vault in Holmes' office became a death trap for many of his lovers. Later, when the Chicago Fire Department tested viscous,

A photo of Holmes Castle.
(*The Holmes-Pitezel Case;* Frank Geyer;
Philadelphia: Publisher's Union, 1896)

musty-smelling oil found on the floor of the vault, they added a small amount of crude petroleum to the mix and were shocked when a lethal vapor wafted forth. Though it appeared harmless, the ensuing mist was capable of paralyzing the nervous system, resulting in almost instantaneous death. A poignant testament to the viciousness of which Holmes was capable was the sad, heartbreakingly small footprint found on the inside of the vault's door when the Castle was searched by Chicago Police. Having gotten the oil on the sole of her foot, a woman had branded the door with a sign of her struggles for life.

The majority of these buoyantly pretty young women died anonymous deaths in Holmes' Castle, but a few were remembered and their stories told during the investigation and trial that followed the killer's arrest.

Julia Smythe Conner, a statuesque beauty almost six feet tall, with lively green eyes and thick chestnut hair, came to the Castle with her

husband in late 1890. Icilius T. "Ned" Conner had dragged his wife and their two-year-old daughter, Pearl, from one failed job to another until they finally sought their fortune in Chicago.

Jeweler Davis who ran the first-floor jewelry store at the Castle. (*Chicago Times-Herald;* July 25, 1895; Courtesy the Abraham Lincoln Presidential Library.)

Excited by a newspaper ad for a qualified jewelry-store manager, Ned braved the cold and applied for the job. He was thrilled when Holmes hired him on the spot with a salary of $12.00 a week, plus room and board for his little family.

The Christmas season was upon them, and the city came alive, redolent in the tangy aroma of pine boughs and glittering with tinsel. Holmes bounded cheerfully into the jewelry store one day to find that the Conners had a visitor – Ned's sister Gertrude. Her lively charm captured Holmes' fascination, and the eighteen-

Dr. H.H. Holmes (*Philadelphia Inquirer;* July, 1895; Courtesy of the Free Library of Philadelphia).

year-old girl was dazzled by the worldly businessman. Gertrude quickly fell under Holmes' spell, and he, apparently, under hers. He soon volunteered to divorce Myrta and marry Gertie, but the ease with which Holmes could discard his family frightened the young woman, and she returned home to Muscatine.

Stinging from her rejection, Holmes apparently sent Gertie home with a poisonous elixir which claimed her life some weeks later.

It is unclear when Julia and Dr. Holmes became lovers, but by March of 1891 they were involved. Holmes fired his drug store cashier and ensconced Julia in her place. The two were not discreet and their

Julia Conner.
(*Chicago Times-Herald;* July 25, 1895; Courtesy the Abraham Lincoln Presidential Library.)

affair was soon common knowledge among regular customers, though Ned seemed blissfully unaware of what was happening right under his nose. After several friends told him what was going on, he was forced to confront his wife. During an ugly row, he threatened to leave Julia if she didn't break it off with Holmes, but she flatly refused. Ned left both his job and his living quarters in the Castle and moved to an apartment, filed for divorce, and secured work with the H. Purdy Company. Not long after the breakup of his marriage, he left Chicago for good. He would never see his little girl again.

Julia had a gay, outgoing personality and her unbridled ambition was shockingly inappropriate for a woman of that era. She insisted that Holmes pay for her to attend the local business school and, following her graduation, hand over the books of his businesses to her.

Ned Connor.
(*Chicago Times-Herald;* **July 25, 1895; Courtesy the Abraham Lincoln Presidential Library.**)

Holmes was quite charmed with Julia's spirit and ambition at first, but he was used to much more sedate and pliant women and felt that Julia had overstepped her boundaries. In November of 1891, Julia became pregnant, and, ignorant of the deadly potential of her lover, demanded Holmes marry her.

When Julia laid her ultimatum at his feet, Holmes coaxed and petted her into submission before proposing that she submit to an abortion. Stunned and horrified, Julia initially refused and the two fought bitterly. But eventually, as always, Holmes got his way and the surgery was scheduled for Christmas Eve.

Haunted by the act she was about to commit, Julia became irritable and hateful, but on December 24th, Holmes had made all the preparations and was ready to perform the surgery. He soothed a distraught Julia, offering to tuck her daughter, Pearl, into bed that night himself. Holmes sneaked off to his office and retrieved a bottle and a cloth before leading the little girl to her bedroom. Wrapped in a shawl, the sobbing and grief-stricken Julia remained huddled against the bedstead to await her lover's return.

Pearl Conner.
(***Chicago Times-Herald;*** **July 25, 1895; Courtesy the Abraham Lincoln Presidential Library.**)

Holmes changed little Pearl into her nightgown, tucked her into bed, and then pulled the cloth from his pocket and drenched it with chloroform. He returned to Julia about fifteen minutes later, reporting that Pearl was sound asleep and wouldn't awaken for some time. In fact, Pearl would never wake up again.

Weeping pitifully, Julia allowed Holmes to lead her down into the bowels of his underground torture chamber. Julia had never been in the cold, damp cellar before, and had no way of knowing that, as Holmes applied ether to ease the pain of the procedure, when she was reunited with her daughter, it would be in the hereafter.

Soon after Julia's death, Holmes learned that a machinist in his employ, Charles M. Chappell, was skilled in rearticulating human skeletons. Chappell was delighted to be of extra service to his boss, and followed Holmes to a dimly-lit room on the second floor. The body of a young woman, which Chappell described as looking like "a jackrabbit that had been skinned by splitting the skin down the face and rolling it back off the entire body." A man of scant means, the $36.00 Holmes offered Chappell to remove the flesh and reassemble the skeleton of the corpse was a true windfall, and he gladly accepted.

After Chappell had finished his work, Holmes sold the skeleton to a local medical school, but its ownership was eventually handed to a Dr. Pauling. The doctor was delighted with his find, as he had never seen a female skeleton of that height – almost six feet!

The new tenants of the Conner's living quarters were surprised to find the place in disarray when first shown the rooms – dried food crusted the dishes and breadcrumbs littered the tablecloth. In the closet, fashionable frocks hung neatly beside a child's dresses, a woman's and child's underwear were arranged tidily in the bureau drawers, and a fetching hat rested on the dresser. Holmes blithely explained that a sudden illness in the family had caused the Conners to rush back home. The new renters, though, were puzzled why the belongings had never been sent for and why the woman would leave without her pretty hat, the child without her shoes.

Later, when called to testify during Holmes trial, Ned Conner would report that, during his stay in the Castle, Holmes had often urged him to take out life insurance, as had his wife. He had refused and appeared shaken by the knowledge of his close brush with death. Ned stated that he had no doubt Holmes had benefited from Julia's death via the insurance route, and though a horrifying thought, maybe his daughter's, as well.

A valuable commodity in Holmes' schemes was his employee, Benjamin F. Pitezel. When Pitezel's drinking began to interfere with his work, Holmes paid to have the man sent to an institution offering a method known as the "gold cure" for alcoholism. Pitezel returned from the Keeley Institute in Dwight, Illinois, sober and rambling on about the beautiful stenographer who worked at the hospital.

Holmes was intrigued by Pitezel's raves about the woman, and offered Emeline Cigrand the job as his private secretary, dangling a salary of $18.00 a week – 50% more than she was currently earning.

An excited Emeline arrived in Chicago in May of 1892, bursting with enthusiasm and ready to seek her fortune. She took a room in a boarding house near the Castle, and Holmes went into overdrive in his efforts to seduce her. Emeline was dizzy with the exciting changes in her life...not just her new job, but Dr. Holmes' attentiveness, as well. He bought her gifts and flowers, took her to see the sights, and escorted her to the theater following expensive dinners in fashionable restaurants downtown. At Marshall Fields he bought her feminine trinkets of all sorts – ribbons, a tortoiseshell comb, and a cameo brooch. Sunday afternoons they strolled around Englewood or wandered through parks on their matching Pope bicycles. Emeline adored her bicycle, her job, and her new beau.

By mid-summer, they were lovers.

The details of their relationship are scant and murky, but the beautiful Emeline grew to expect Holmes to marry her. She confronted Holmes in the fall of 1892 and was delighted and surprised when

Emeline Cigrand. (*Chicago Times-Herald;* **July 25, 1895; Courtesy the Abraham Lincoln Presidential Library.**)

he readily capitulated. Not only did he agree but encouraged Emeline to spread the joyous news.

The young woman was thrilled about her upcoming nuptials, and this effusiveness showed in the letters she wrote to her family. She regaled them with tales of his kindness and generosity, of his fine manners and gentlemanly ways, and of his lofty position and wealth. They were, she gushed, planning to honeymoon in Europe, telling younger sister Philomena Ida that Holmes was the heir of a British lord. She would, Emeline continued, have the opportunity to meet her new father-in-law on their honeymoon, and added that the newlyweds might well decide to settle in England permanently.

In early October of 1892, Emeline welcomed her cousins, Dr. & Mrs. B. J. Cigrand, to Chicago, where they toured the Castle's first-floor shops and Holmes' third-floor office. The other portions of the Castle were, she said, private quarters. Emeline was disappointed when Dr. Cigrand was not wildly impressed as she had hoped, but downright critical of the shoddy workmanship and materials of the building.

Whether Holmes simply never mentioned his existing family or told Emeline he was divorced, Myrta seemed never to have been brought into the situation. Emeline was beside herself with joy when Holmes handed her twelve engraved cards that November to formally announce their wedding.

The week the two were to be married, Holmes and Emeline were in his office, ostensibly making wedding plans, when he asked her to fetch something from the huge vault. When the door closed behind her, Emeline was not at first concerned. But panic soon set in, and the young woman pleaded and sobbed, begging for her life, for hours. Holmes had the means to end her life quickly, but needed the sounds of her terror to excite him and provide sexual release.

Emeline was never seen again...not around the Castle or anywhere else. Her family received wedding announcements the middle of December and read the happy news:

Mr. Robert Phelps

Miss Emeline Cigrand

Married;

Wed

Wednesday, December 7

1892

Chicago

The use of the Phelps alias in these announcements was never explained, and how Holmes justified the deception to his "fiancé" remains a mystery.

Just after the New Year, LaSalle Medical School acquired a beautiful anatomical treasure – a perfect female skeleton purchased from Dr. H. H. Holmes.

Most accounts of what went on in Holmes' Castle come directly from the killer's memoirs, *Holmes Own Story*. His words need to be read with the full knowledge of the man's compulsion for lying and deception. Dishonesty was so firmly rooted, so second-nature to Holmes, he seems incapable of recognizing, let alone telling, the truth.

Into this atmosphere came Minnie Williams, easily the most significant of his conquests in that she is such a feature player in his explanations and confessions following arrest. Holmes' statements about how and when he met Minnie are murky. He said he was unsure if he met her in New York City, where he was known as Edward Hatch, or later, in Boston, where he used the alias of Harry Gordon. He has even claimed that they met in Mississippi in 1886, and, at one point, denied knowing the woman at all until she showed up at the Castle looking for a job. However they met, Minnie *did* become his private secretary in March of 1893.

Plump and short, Minnie was an innocent and naïve young lady with curly brown hair that framed her round face. She was sweet and simple, with a pleasant demeanor, and Pat Quinlan immediately noticed the contrast between Minnie and the other women with whom Holmes had become intimate. What attracted Holmes to Minnie was his *other* compulsive need – money. The woman was heir to a small fortune, having been orphaned at the age of six. Killed in a train accident, the loss of Minnie's father left his wife heartbroken, and she died shortly thereafter. An uncle in Dallas took Minnie in and fell under her charm, treating

Minnie Williams. (*Chicago Times-Herald;* **July 25, 1895; Courtesy the Abraham Lincoln Presidential Library.**)

her as his own. A younger sister, Nannie, went to another uncle in Jackson, Mississippi.

From a family of means, Minnie was sent to Boston Conservatory of Music and Elocution when she turned twenty. Her future looked bright, but before she graduated, her world turned upside down. Her beloved uncle died, leaving her the heir to his $40,000 estate in Fort Worth. Grief stricken, the young woman finished school and took some time thereafter to travel.

Within a few months of Minnie's arrival in Chicago, Dr. Holmes was sharing her bed at the Castle. Somehow, once again, Myrta was explained away to yet another lover's satisfaction. Holmes and Minnie set up house at 1220 Wrightwood Avenue after creditors began to circle like vultures around the building at Sixty-third and Wallace. Ingenuous Minnie gladly signed over her Fort Worth property to her beloved's control, since they were soon to be married, anyway. Holmes mulled over the options and possibilities of this windfall, pondering how to turn the property into cold hard cash and how to deal with that other loose end, Minnie's sister Nannie.

Throughout this entire period, while overseeing things at the Castle, Holmes made frequent trips to Wilmette to visit Myrta and Lucy. It was a juggling act at which he became very adept.

The two sisters bonded following the death of Minnie's guardian, and they clung together desperately to retain some feeling of family. When it became necessary to claim her inheritance, Minnie asked Nannie to accompany her. Nannie fell in love with Fort Worth and, over Minnie's protestations, remained there when the older sister had to return to Boston in 1890. They remained in touch, happily visiting each other in their respective cities from time to time.

Like the young women before her, Minnie raved and rhapsodized about her fiancé and their approaching wedding while Holmes was already plotting just how to deal with Nannie. He was certain Minnie could not meet with an "unfortunate accident" without arousing the suspicions of her sister. Brilliant sociopath that he was, Holmes suggested Minnie invite Nannie to come and see the World's Fair that summer and get to know her future brother-in-law.

Equally-innocent Nannie was captivated by Holmes when they met at the railway station, won over by his warmth and unflagging charm. Holmes insisted on being the gentleman and maintaining a correct appearance for the girl, so he moved back into the Castle in order to accommodate his future sister-in-law. For her part, Nannie was enthralled with "Brother Harry."

Holmes had treated Minnie to the delights of the Columbian Exposition already, but the couple took the awe-stricken Nannie to the

World's Fair on July 3rd. Nannie was enchanted with everything about the White City, from the Ferris wheel to Thomas Edison's Tower of Light, and the display of the largest gold nugget in the world. She was enraptured and her letters back home to her uncle in Mississippi vibrated with the glamour and glitz of the Fair, Chicago, and especially her 'Brother Harry.'

Nannie Williams. (*Chicago Times-Herald;* July 25, 1895; Courtesy the Abraham Lincoln Presidential Library.)

Nannie aspired to being an artist, and was pleased and excited when Holmes carried on about her talent in that venue. He encouraged the giddy young woman to stay and study art, and she happily agreed. To her uncle, she gushed about promises from Brother Harry of a trip to Milwaukee, New York, and Maine for himself and "his girls" in the near future. He might, she wrote breathlessly, even take them abroad. The thought of seeing London and Paris, and studying in those lauded strongholds of the arts, excited her to the point of dizziness. She assured her uncle he need never worry about his beloved ward ever again, not personally nor financially, for her new brother would care for her.

One autumn afternoon, Holmes took Nannie on yet another tour of his impressive Castle. Minnie stayed back at the apartment to finish some housework. Everyone was gone for the Thanksgiving holiday, and the deserted building into which he led Nannie echoed its emptiness as they climbed the stairs to the third floor.

He must, Holmes said, do a bit of business before they returned to the apartment. He settled Nannie comfortably in his office before seating himself at his desk. After a brief interval, he looked up, seemingly distracted, and asked Nannie to retrieve something from the vault. Once she was inside, Holmes quietly moved from his chair and closed the door behind her.

One of the last acts Nannie would perform in this world was to leave a painfully small, poignant reminder of her presence – her footprint on the door of the vault as she fought for her life.

Minnie was surprised when Holmes returned without her sister, but he quickly explained that Nannie had been suddenly stricken with homesickness to see her guardian and he had taken her immediately to the train depot. She had plenty of clothing and toiletries back home and needn't return with her packed luggage. After all, she planned to be back shortly after Christmas.

Unfortunately, Minnie accepted Holmes' explanation, and when he suggested the two of them get away from Chicago for Thanksgiving, as well, she bundled up what she would need. Holmes had his valise packed and ready. The lovesick Minnie accompanied Holmes to a small house he had secured near Momence, Illinois. He plied the unsuspecting woman with tea, lacing the drink liberally with poison, and buried her in the dank, musty darkness of the cellar.

When explaining Nannie's disappearance later, Holmes claimed that Minnie had grown jealous of his attentiveness to her sister. In a rage, he said, Minnie brought a chair down on Nannie's head, killing her instantly. Appalled by her own actions, Minnie fled Chicago and Holmes hadn't seen her since.

The Williams sisters were now just a lovely memory.

"Upon reaching Fort Worth, I found that some to whom money was owing had filed mechanics' and furnishers' liens against the property...."

H. H. Holmes

Chapter Six

The Beginning of the End

An unencumbered Holmes began to sort through the dead Williams' sisters belongings and was pleasantly surprised to find an insurance policy in their favor on their brother's life. With the policies he had taken out on the two women, that extra bonus would set him up quite nicely for his planned trip to Texas. Besides, the buzzards were circling the Castle, and his hopes of remaining a free man in Chicago were dwindling rapidly.

But before he left, he arranged to have the Castle torched, most probably by Pat Quinlan, while Holmes himself was on a short business trip. Only the top story burned, but he had $25,000 in fire insurance spread among four different companies and upon his return, set about trying to collect. His days in Chicago were numbered, and he planned to leave with as much cash as possible.

Touring the charred building with Holmes, Fire Inspector F. G. Cowie, who was familiar with his companion's dubious business practices, told Holmes that the fire was highly suspicious. It seemed to have started in several different spots on the top floor at the same instant.

News of the suspicious fire jarred his creditors into action, and they converged on him en masse. Dozens of them collaborated to hire an attorney, and with strength in numbers, attempted to recover the money due them. The attorney showed up at the Castle and issued an ultimatum – either Holmes immediately pay the $50,000 owed his clients or a warrant would be sworn out for his arrest.

As soon as the attorney left with an effusive promise of the requested payment, Holmes left town and journeyed to Colorado to pay the brother of the Williams sisters a visit. The last time Holmes was seen in Chicago was late November, 1893.

While in Colorado the year before, Holmes once again fell in love, and the good doctor had never managed to master self denial. Georgiana Yoke was a beautiful woman with blue eyes so large that one description called them "almost disfiguring." She was twenty-three years old and quite petite, with sharp, sculpted features. Unfortunately, she was also in love with her new beau, a man she knew as Henry Mansfield Howard. Holmes set about winning her confidence and trust with a vengeance.

The weather in Colorado was numbingly cold and snow turned the city of Denver into a winter wonderland. With the Christmas decorations glittering and the sound of carols in the cold air, it was an enchanting time for romance to flourish. After killing the Williams sisters' brother, Holmes used a power of attorney secured early in his relationship with Minnie and Nannie to collect the insurance payoff in their names. Newly flush with cash, he proceeded to the frosty town to court his most recent lady love. They had met in 1892, when Holmes had been in town promoting his ABC Copier Company, the only legitimate business he ever operated. On that trip, he met Georgiana at Schlesinger & Meyers Department Store.

Now, sad and grief-stricken, Holmes explained to Georgiana that his beloved uncle had died, and he needed to travel to Texas to take care of his estate. Georgiana happily agreed when Holmes suggested they use the trip as a honeymoon. The jubilant couple was married in Denver on January 9, 1894, with the Rev. Wilcox presiding. Blissful and glowing, it was obvious to the minister that Georgiana was completely besotted with her equally doting husband.

The first week was magical for Georgiana, everything a new bride could want. The rumble and gentle sway of the railroad car rocked them to sleep each night, wrapped in one another's arms. They drank fine wine in the dining car and ate the best beef steaks. Everyone onboard was delighted with the newlyweds and they with them. A few days later, the couple arrived in Fort Worth, beaming and deliriously happy.

Holmes checked them into a hotel under the alias of H. M. Pratt, telling his puzzled new bride that the subterfuge was necessary as squatters had settled on his uncle's ranch and he did not want to alert them to his presence. With deep solemnity he assured her that he was confident of soon laying claim to his rightful inheritance, but the ruse was necessary for the time being. They were, after all, in Texas, he said, where gunplay was often used to settle disputes. Georgiana embraced Holmes, illiciting promises from him to be safe in his dealings. It would be nearly a year before she learned the shocking truth about her "husband."

With Ben Pitezel at his side, a cheerful Holmes strode into the Tarrant County Court House to file the deeds signed over to him by Minnie. For whatever reason, Holmes then transferred ownership of the property to Benton T. Lyman, the alias that Pitezel was using at the time. The two men then began to entertain ambitious schemes for their newly-acquired property. As a result, in the chill of the dying winter, Holmes and Pitezel began construction on yet another Castle... a duplicate of the monstrous structure in Chicago.

Beguiling local merchants, Holmes regaled them with insinuations of his wealth and of his ambitious plans. Producing the deed he had just acquired as collateral, they eagerly gave him the materials and equipment he needed on credit. He also managed to bilk $20,000 from various local banks.

Soon the drum of hammers and the whine of saws were heard coming from his property. Georgiana wandered down often to check construction, her mind spinning with the raucous sound of tools and sharp smell of sawdust. She was joyous beyond expression – newly married to a wealthy and successful, not to mention very handsome, husband and soon to be proprietress of a marvelous, enormous hotel. The clop of horses hooves and the rattle of wagons bringing materials and crews were thrilling, for they were building *her* future...hers and Mr. Howard's.

Just as he had in Chicago, Holmes secured materials and furnishings on credit and issued phony checks for the labor. With his cocky, invincible demeanor, Holmes never shied away from risk. Now he became downright reckless and began to make mistakes. While strolling with Georgiana, he spied a freight car loaded with pedigreed horses destined for a Fort Worth ranch and somehow managed to divert the shipment to Chicago. Horse theft being a hanging crime in Texas, the trio fled the state, but not together.

Georgiana was told they were once again on ABC Copier business, which Holmes had been neglecting, and that Lyman (Pitezel) would oversee construction of their grand hotel. In truth, both men needed to escape Texas to avoid prosecution for horse theft, and the building project underway in Fort Worth was simply abandoned. Georgiana was never aware that Pitezel was always nearby, having left Fort Worth on the same day as she and Holmes.

The three traveled eastward, to Denver, Memphis, Philadelphia, New York, and finally ended up in St. Louis, Missouri. Again using the Henry Mansfield Howard alias, Holmes acquired a small pharmacy for a modest down payment, promising to pay the balance within thirty days. Holmes visited Merrill Drug Company, his prosperous-looking appearance winning the confidence of salesmen, and soon his little drug store was fully stocked.

But Holmes now pushed his luck.

He immediately sold the store, along with the inventory, giving the buyer a fraudulent bill of sale in the name of a Mr. Brown. When Merrill Drug Company came to collect, Holmes said that, alas, he was no longer the proprietor, and they should take the matter up with "Mr. Brown."

Holmes had no reason to believe that the people at Merrill Drug Company would react to the scam any differently than the folks back in Chicago had. This assumption was the first of a few bad decisions that would eventually land Holmes on the gallows at Moyamensing Prison in Philadelphia. On July 19, 1894, Merrill filed charges and the St. Louis police arrested Holmes for fraud.

Georgiana was devastated. Her husband couldn't be guilty of these crimes he had been charged with, and she was quite indignant at the blatant miscarriage of justice.

∾

A handsome bandit, Marion Hedgepeth, known as the "Gentleman Robber," was Holmes' cellmate in the St. Louis Jail. William A. Pinkerton, founder of the famous detective agency, would say that "[Hedgepeth was] one of the really bad men of the Old West. He was one of the worst characters I ever knew of. He was a bad man clear through."

The deed to her Fort Worth property was still in the name of
Minnie Williams' uncle and aunt, Charles & Dora Brogdon, when
it was transferred to Ben Pitezel's alias, Benton T. Lyman.
(From Tarrant County Clerk's records).

**Holmes shared Marion Hedgepeth's jail cell in St. Louis
for only a few days before Georgiana posted his bail.
(*The Chicago Times;* August, 1894; Courtesy of the
Abraham Lincoln Presidential Library)**

In his day, Hedgepeth was every bit as notorious as Jesse James was in his. He left his birthplace of Prairie Home, Missouri, as a teenager, and by the time he turned twenty, was already wanted in Wyoming, Colorado, and Montana for a variety of crimes ranging from cattle rustling to bank robbery.

"The fastest gun in the West," they said, after Hedgepeth managed, while being covered with a rifle by one of his enemies, to draw his pistol and kill the man before his foe could even pull the rifle's trigger. Tall, with wavy black hair and dark eyes, Hedgepeth was vain and dressed like an Eastern "dandy." Wearing his favorite duds – a blue suit, striped cravat, brown derby, and spit-polished shoes – newspapers named him

"The Handsome Bandit." But he was as ruthless as any outlaw in crime's annals.

It was with Marion Hedgepeth that Holmes made his second, and fatal, mistake.

He and his partner, Holmes told Hedgepeth, were planning to run an insurance scam he had used several times before. His friend, Pitezel, would insure his own life for $10,000, and then they would convince the insurance company he was dead by substituting a body similar to Pitezel's. Would Hedgepeth know

Marion Hedgepeth, the Gentleman Robber, was Holmes' cellmate in St. Louis. (*Philadelphia Inquirer*; April 26, 1896; Courtesy of the Free Library of Philadelphia).

of an attorney who could assist them in this endeavor? Holmes would gladly pay him $500 after the insurance settlement. Hedgepeth agreed and Holmes instructed Georgiana to contact the attorney. Georgiana then posted bail, freeing her husband after ten days of incarceration.

At this point, Georgiana began to wonder about the man she had married, but felt she had no recourse, which motivated her to tamp down any doubts she was experiencing.

Holmes and Ben visited with the Pitezel family, who lived in St. Louis, to lay the groundwork for their planned fraud. A mousy, exhausted woman, Carrie Pitezel didn't have the energy to protest, certainly not with the demands of her brood of five children, one just an infant. She reluctantly agreed to go along with the plan.

Pitezel came reeling in drunk one night when his oldest daughter, Dessie, was the only soul still awake. He fawned over her, his potent breath hot upon her face, his unwashed body reeking, and instructed her to "disregard any reports of my death." Dessie dismissed her father's drunken ramblings, this being only one of many times drink had caused him to act peculiarly.

Dessie Pitezel (left), with her mother, Carrie.
(*Philadelphia Inquirer;* April 26, 1896; Courtesy
of the Free Library of Philadelphia).

Exhausted and anxious following Holmes arrest in St. Louis, Georgiana wanted nothing more than to leave all the bad experiences behind them. Not to worry, her husband reassured her. They were all just terrible misunderstandings. He proposed yet another trip on ABC Copier business to Philadelphia, and Georgiana leaped at the suggestion. The slightly-disenchanted bride left with her husband and arrived in Pennsylvania on Sunday, July 29, 1894.

It would be Holmes' downfall that he gave no further thought to the promise made to his cellmate in the St. Louis jail.

"It will be understood that from the first hour of our
acquaintance...I intended to kill [Pitezel]...."

H. H. Holmes

Chapter Seven

The City of Brotherly Love

Three weary travelers – Holmes, Georgiana, and Pitezel – arrived
at the noisy Philadelphia and Reading Railroad station, where the cloy-
ing stench of unwashed bodies mingled with that of stale urine. They
quickly scurried off to find rooms and rest up from their journey. The
next day, Holmes ventured out into the bustling city to locate an office
from which to stage his newest insurance fraud. He chose a two-and-
a-half story, red brick house in a decaying neighborhood just across the
street from the railroad station via which he and his companions had
arrived. Number 1316 on Callowhill sported naked metal poles jutting
up from the concrete, their purpose to support an awning which had
long since departed. On August 17, 1894, Pitezel strung a white sheet
across the front window with bright red letters screaming the arrival of
B. F. Perry, Patents Bought and Sold.

Pitezel did everything in his power to discourage clients to approach him, including spending most of his time at a nearby saloon. But, Eugene Smith, a carpenter and inventor who lived on Rhoads Street, felt his heart jump when he first spied the sign. Having built and patented a saw set, a device that sharpened saw blades, the arrival of Mr. Perry seemed quite fortuitous. Determined to follow through, Smith continued to wander by the business until he finally found Pitezel inside. He hurried in and enthusiastically described for "Mr. Perry" the fantastic abilities of his wonderful saw set, convinced he was on his way to prosperity.

Pitezel responded to Smith's vigorous endorsement of his invention and asked to see the model saw set. Smith proudly presented his machine the next day, explaining to Pitezel how it worked. During this demonstration, a well-dressed and immaculately groomed gentleman entered the store, strode to the foot of the stairs, and gestured for Pitezel to join him. After a brief conference on the second floor, the men returned and Pitezel dismissed Smith.

The inventor Smith was beside himself with excitement and hope, so he kept checking the shop for indications it was open for business. On September 3rd, he found the door ajar and went inside, discovering his beloved saw set unattended on the counter in the unlocked shop. The room, which had been pin neat on his earlier visits, was messy, and Smith called out for its owner. With no response from his greeting, he sat down to wait for Pitezel to return. In the middle of the floor sat a chair, an odd spot, he thought, for one to place a chair, but hardly ominous. Pitezel's tie, collar, and vest hung from a nail near the

No. 1316 Callowhill St., Philadelphia, where Pitezel opened his "patent office." (*The Holmes-Pitezel Case*; **Frank Geyer; Philadelphia: Publisher's Union, 1896**)

stairs, which also struck him as odd. He idly wondered if Pitezel might have a second set of outer wear, since gentlemen did not sashay forth amongst the general public without being properly dressed. Loath as he was to leave his precious saw set in such a vulnerable situation, Smith left after waiting about an hour.

The inventor returned bright and early the next day, hopeful of catching Pitezel so they might have a chat. The door was as he had left it – closed, but not locked. The chair in the middle of the floor was right where he had left it; the tie, collar, and vest still hung near the stairway. Now Smith became alarmed. It looked as though nobody had been in the room since he had left it yesterday, and a vague, unpleasant odor now permeated the room.

Smith decided to investigate the premises and climbed the stairs to the second floor. The first room he entered had only a single, unmade bed. What he saw in the second room, however, caused his heart to stop. His mind struggled to register the decomposing corpse. With its red hair, mustache and goatee, and wearing the pants that matched the vest downstairs, Smith had no doubt that the discolored face and bloated body was that of "Mr. Perry." Swollen and dark, the tongue jutted from his mouth like a crocus in springtime. A corncob pipe filled with tobacco lay near the body next to a burned match. Shards of glass from a clear bottle sparkled on the floor, and the fetid smell intensified as he drew nearer to the corpse, causing him to gag.

The inventor fled the shop, rushing to the Buttonwood Street police station as though hounds were on his heels. Two officers left the station with Smith, and their only stop on the way back to the Callowhill house was to pick up a doctor. When the quartet entered the shop, they followed the stench to Pitezel's putrefying corpse on the second floor.

The doctor knelt beside the body, clamping a handkerchief over his nose against the smell, and assessed Pitezel's condition. The front of the man's shirt, as well as his mustache, was singed. A clutch of bottles containing cleaning solution, benzine, chloroform, and ammonia were perched on the mantle. The scene looked like an obvious accident that might have occurred while the dead man was experimenting with the volatile liquids and, unthinking, lit his pipe too close to the fluids. The doctor, as well as the two police officers, agreed it was an accidental demise.

Conveniently located directly behind the patent office was the city morgue and Pitezel's body was taken there for autopsy, which was performed that afternoon. The results concurred with the doctor and officer's conclusion at the scene...at least for the time being. The death

**A parking lot now occupies the block where the Callowhill house stood.
(Snavely Collection)**

certificate stated that death was due to chloroform poisoning, and upon
Smith's recognition of the dead man's clothing, assumed to be the patent dealer. No facial identification could be made due to the advanced
decomposition.

A September 5th coroner's inquest resulted in the jurors agreeing
with that scenario, since the precise cause of death presented was "congestion of the lungs, caused by the inhalation of flame or of chloroform,
or other poisonous drug." A small article about "Perry's" death in the
Philadelphia papers was picked up by the wire services, setting the final
wheels in motion that would eventually result in Holmes' hanging. The
body of Benjamin Pitezel, alias B. F. Perry, went unclaimed and eventually ended up buried in Potter's Field.

About the same time as Pitezel's interment, the Fidelity Mutual Life
Insurance Company in Philadelphia received an odd telegram from
George B. Stadden, their St. Louis office manager. It stated that "the

B. F. Perry, found dead in Philadelphia, is claimed to be B. F. Pitezel, who is insured on 044145. Investigate before remains leave there."

Carrie Pitezel's attorney, Jeptha D. Howe, the lawyer recommended to Holmes by Marion Hedgepeth, promptly sent a telegram to the headquarters, as well. That missive also claimed Perry was Pitezel. Howe informed the insurance company he was now making arrangements with the widow to come to Philadelphia and identify the body and claim the insurance payoff.

Claim manager O. LaForrest Perry immediately secured the file on policy number 044145, which had been issued less than a year earlier on Pitezel's life for $10,000. That amount of gold-backed money in today's economy would amount to around $100,000, a substantial payout. What piqued Perry's suspicion, besides the short time the policy had been in effect, was the fact the last premium of $157.50 had been telegraphed to the office on the last day of the policy's grace period – August 9, 1894.

Holmes arrived at Fidelity Mutual's Philadelphia office on September 20th, claiming the body as that of his friend Benjamin F. Pitezel. He pulled out the stops, plying the management with his charm, sophistication, and frank honesty. Holmes smoothed over the use of an alias by explaining that Pitezel had been in financial trouble in Tennessee a few months back. L. G. Fouse, Fidelity Mutual's president, was satisfied with Holmes' explanation and began the tedious legal steps to have Pitezel's body exhumed for identification. Fouse was not satisfied the body in Potter's Field was

L. G. Fouse, President of the Fidelity Mutual Insurance Company. (*Philadelphia Inquirer;* **April 12, 1896; Courtesy of the Free Library of Philadelphia**).

Benjamin Pitezel, but he did agree that Pitezel and Perry were one and the same man.

Jeptha Howe arrived in Philadelphia armed with Mrs. Pitezel's power of attorney and several letters Ben had written her while using the Perry alias. Due to Carrie's poor health, one of the children had to accompany Howe to view the body, but the oldest daughter, Dessie, was needed in St. Louis to help care for baby Wharton. Therefore, accompanying the lawyer was fifteen-year-old Alice.

A party comprised of Deputy Coroner Dugan, coroner's physician Dr. Mattern, a Dr. Hill, President Fouse, claims manager O. LeForrest Perry, inventor Eugene Smith, Alice Pitezel, Jeptha Howe, and Holmes headed to Potter's Field to look at the corpse. Identification would be made based on physical anomalies – a mole on the back of Pitezel's neck, a scar on his leg, a bruised thumb, and "certain peculiarities of the teeth."

In the close, gloomy woodshed, the decomposing corpse lay on a table, concealed by a white sheet. The stink of rotting flesh was nauseating. Dr. Mattern pulled on rubber gloves and removed the sheet to search for the identifying marks. Completely blackened by that time, the body would not give up its secrets easily, and Mattern failed to find that which he sought. At that point, Holmes donned gloves, retrieved a scalpel from his pocket, and cut the mole from Pitezel's neck. Lifting the body's pants leg, he pointed to the scar, visible through the discoloration. But finding the bruised thumb was a quest that would not be realized due to the darkened skin.

The body was again swathed in sheets, with only the teeth visible, and Alice was led into the shed.

Perry asked her, "Are these your father's teeth?"

Alice, sobbing pitifully, confirmed that they were.

An anxious Dr. Holmes brought Alice to the office of coroner Samuel H. Ashbridge the next day, where the two gave their sworn statements regarding the identification of the body. Fidelity Mutual Life's officers met, agreeing that the identity was complete, and paid the claim immediately, less the expenses incurred in the procedure. A beaming Jeptha Howe left the insurance office with a check for $9,715.85.

When Carrie Pitezel arrived in Philadelphia to claim Ben's body and insurance money, she stepped from the train into the crisp fall morning and was surprised to see not only her attorney, Howe, but Holmes as well, deep in conversation. Howe congratulated her on the settlement and gave her a small amount of the money for her and the children's immediate needs.

**Alice Pitezel in the shack at Potter's Field, identifying
her father. Holmes stands beside her.
(*Philadelphia Inquirer*; Sept. 23, 1895; Courtesy
of the Free Library of Philadelphia).**

A glib and deceptive explanation from Holmes, who, after all, was her friend, convinced a reluctant Carrie to allow two of the younger children to remain with him.

Heavy-hearted, Carrie returned to St. Louis with Dessie and baby Wharton, not knowing they would soon be all that was left of the six people she loved so dearly.

Several letters regarding the Pitezel case crossed the desks at Fidelity Mutual in the next few weeks. Some of these, written by Carrie and Alice Pitezel, as well as Holmes, expressed gratitude for the expedited settlement on the policy. But it was a letter sent to the St. Louis police department that would knock the final prop from beneath Holmes' lofty ego. He had totally forgotten, or decided to disregard, the promise he made to his cellmate a few months earlier. The letter, written by Marion Hedgepeth, the infamous criminal enjoying the hospitality of the City of St. Louis' prison, was addressed to Superintendent Harrigan and tumbled Holmes' house of cards.

Harrigan dispatched a messenger to the Fidelity Mutual office in St. Louis on October 9th, saying that the superintendent thought someone should hurry to his office. William Gary, Fidelity Mutual's detective, responded to the message. Harrigan wordlessly handed Gary the letter, which read:

"When H. M. Howard was in here some months ago, he told me he had a scheme by which he could make $10,000, and he needed some lawyer who could be trusted, and said if I could get him one he would see that I got $500 for it. I then told him Jeptha D. Howe could be trusted. He then told me that B. F. Pitezel's life was insured for $10,000, and that Pitezel and him were going to work the insurance company, and just how they were going to do it; even going into minute details; that he was an expert at it, as he had worked it before, and that being a druggist, he could easily deceive the insurance company by having Pitezel fix himself up according to his directions and appear that he was mortally wounded by an explosion, and then put a corpse in place of Pitezel, and then have it identified as that of Pitezel.

"I did not take much stock in what he told me, until a few days after he went out on bond, when Lawyer Howe came to me and told me that Howard had come and laid the whole plot open to him...The insurance company, he said, was the Fidelity Mutual of Philadelphia.

"When notice appeared in the Globe Democrat of the death of B. F. Perry, Howe came down at once and told me that it was a matter of a few days until we would have the money, and that the only thing that might keep the company from paying it at once, was the fact that Howard and Pitezel were so hard up they could not pay the premium on the policy until a day or two before it was due, and then had to send it by telegram, and that the company might claim that they did not get the money until after the lapse of the policy. But the company made no such claim, and so Howe and a little girl (I think Pitezel's daughter) went to Philadelphia and succeeded in identifying and having the body recognized as that of B. F. Pitezel.

"It is hardly worthwhile to say that I never got the $500 that Howard held out to me...Please excuse this poor writing as I have written this in a hurry and have to write on a book placed on my knee. This and a lot more I am willing to swear to."

Gary had always thought the case questionable, and Hedgepeth's letter confirmed his nagging suspicions. Harrigan told the insurance detective his police force had been looking for the man, Howard, ever since he jumped bail. The superintendent handed Gary a picture taken when Holmes was arrested, and the detective identified the person immediately as none other than Dr. Holmes.

Even with all this evidence, Fidelity Mutual was not anxious to reopen the case and stonewalled Gary for a while, most likely from wounded pride, not wanting to admit they had been duped. Claims representative Perry agreed with Gary that the case should be given another look, but the top brass argued that Hedgepeth was, after all, a criminal and had made the whole thing up. But stumped as to how the bandit knew of the late payment being telegraphed, they finally relented.

Perry and Gary immediately began trying to find Carrie Pitezel, who had since left town. The only members of her family to leave with her were Dessie and baby Wharton. Though the two men had not seen Carrie's husband around, they had seen Mr. Howard, who was now in Philadelphia with the other three Pitezel children.

Superintendent Harrigan mentioned that Holmes' wife had bailed him out, but his description of the young woman who freed the man was completely different from what they already knew of Holmes' wife, Myrta, in Illinois. Now the authorities were convinced the doctor was not only a fraud, but a bigamist, as well. However, they were convinced of Georgiana's ignorance to the existence of Holmes' other wife in Illinois.

A very loyal Myrta would give the men nothing to work with. They thought her devotion might flag when told of the new wife, but she seemed blasé and unconcerned when given that information. They were fairly sure that Myrta was as *aware* of her husband's darker acts as Georgiana was *unaware* of them.

They struck gold, though, with the Chicago Police Department, who had warrants out for Holmes' arrest under several different aliases for a number of frauds, with Pitezel running a close second on their wanted list. Their interest in Holmes was greater because of his connection with a string of young women who had gone missing, among them Minnie Williams.

At this time, the Castle in Chicago was vacant and locked up except for what shops still remained on the first floor. There was a buzz around the neighborhood now about the people who had been seen entering, but never leaving, the building. Holmes' creditors were hassling over how to divvy up the property and rumors were flying.

With an ever-widening geographical area involved, Gary and Perry decided they needed an investigative agency with a national scope.

They hired the Pinkertons.

"[All my kindnesses] were steps taken to gain [Pitezel's] confidence and that of his family so when the time was ripe, they would the more readily fall into my hands."

H. H. Holmes

Chapter Eight

On the Run

Holmes boarded the train to leave Philadelphia with the two Pitezel children. Though he stayed in Fort Worth, Denver, and St. Louis for several weeks before moving on, having become something of a vagabond, he now began to literally live a nomadic existence. Holmes masterminded a dizzying journey, one so purposely complex and aggressive that authorities would find it difficult, if not impossible, to reconstruct.

Alice was waiting on the train platform in Indianapolis with a clerk from the Stubbins Hotel when Holmes stepped out, prodded her into a Pullman, and reunited the three siblings. Alice was ecstatic to see her brother and sister, and they to see her, and the three huddled together in their seats, giggling and chattering.

They arrived in Cincinnati quite late on September 28th. Holmes ushered the cranky and exhausted children to the Atlantic House, a cheap hotel near the station, and registered as a family under the name Alexander E. Cook. With a kind and attentive demeanor, Holmes had won the trust of the children, and there was no protest the next day when he again moved them to the Bristol Hotel. He announced that he was taking Howard along with him to run an errand, tenderly soothing the girls' anxiety over being separated, even for a short time, from their brother.

On that Saturday morning, J. C. Thomas was seated behind the desk at his real estate agency when the bell over the door jingled the arrival of a client. A dapper gentleman, meticulously groomed and clothed, walked in with a small, very shabbily dressed boy at his side. He couldn't help noticing the contrast between the two but still assumed they were father and son.

With a smile and a confident handshake, Holmes introduced himself as A. C. Hayes and said he was looking for a small house to rent. Hayes' excitement and agitation jibed with his statement that he was in a rush, so Thomas leafed through his files and found exactly what the man needed. Holmes paid fifteen dollars in advance, took the key to 305 Poplar Street, asked where the nearest used furniture store might be, took Howard by the hand, and left Thomas' office.

Later that day, Holmes was at the house to accept the delivery of a huge cylindrical stove, far too large to be practical for such a small place, a fact not missed by neighbor Henrietta Hill. A small boy skipped and

Alice Pitezel
(*The Holmes-Pitezel Case*; Frank Geyer;
Philadelphia: Publisher's Union, 1896)

Nettie Pitezel
(*The Holmes-Pitezel Case*; Frank Geyer;
Philadelphia: Publisher's Union, 1896)

hopped around the tiny yard, doing everything he could to ward off boredom. Miss Hill was also puzzled by the fact that no other furniture was delivered – only that enormous oven.

Distraught, Holmes paced the floor and wrung his hands, trying to make a decision about Howard. The house wasn't all that isolated and he had noticed the nosy neighbor's interest in his presence. Should anyone ask later on, she would most certainly remember his activities that afternoon. Loath to do so, but with no other choice, Holmes scrapped his plans.

Howard Pitezel
(*The Holmes-Pitezel Case*; Frank Geyer;
Philadelphia: Publisher's Union, 1896)

In an attempt to breed goodwill and dash any suspicions she might have, Holmes appeared at Miss Hill's door the next morning and, telling her his business plans had changed and he would not be staying, offered the stove as a gift. He couldn't drag it with him in his travels, and he was anxious for someone to be able to benefit from its warmth and comfort, he said.

In order to insure their affection for him, Holmes took the Pitezel children to the Cincinnati Zoo later that day. Chattering and skipping, running and laughing, the three Pitezels had a marvelous time with "Uncle Harry." Enchanted with the ostriches, captivated by the monkeys, in awe of the giraffes, and alarmed by the lions and tigers, the children were irrepressible. And Holmes looked for all the world like a doting guardian to spectators, who would never dream that his true plans for these children were so malicious. The stay in Cincinnati set the tone for all the cities and towns through which Holmes would drag the children over the next few weeks.

The Poplar Street House in Cincinnati
(*The Holmes-Pitezel Case;* **Frank Geyer; Philadelphia: Publisher's Union, 1896)**

In Indianapolis, he took rooms at a hotel in close proximity to the Circle Park Hotel where he had left Georgiana while on his "business trip."

On Monday, October 1st, he moved the children to the Circle House, the boarding house that would be their temporary home. Though he wanted very much to stay with them, Holmes said, he needed to return to St. Louis to fetch Carrie, Dessie, and baby Wharton, and offered to take letters back to their mother.

In reality, Holmes reunited with Georgiana, who waited at the Circle Park Hotel. She joyously threw herself into his arms, but her happiness was to be short lived. He had only returned, Holmes said, because he could not go another day without holding and kissing her, but alas, he had to leave right away to resume his business meetings.

Holmes returned to St. Louis and escorted Carrie Pitezel to Jeptha Howe's office to collect her insurance settlement. The two men exchanged bitter words when Howe attempted to retain half of the money as his fee, which, he said, was customary. Howe eventually settled for $2,500 plus his expenses to Philadelphia. An extremely grateful Carrie took the proffered funds and put them into her bag. Holmes quickly hustled her to the bank to deposit her cash.

However, once there, Holmes took Carrie's bag and carefully counted out $5,000, which he said Pitezel owed him to retire a loan. He left Carrie briefly to visit one of the teller windows and returned to give her a cancelled note for $16,000, drawn on the Fort Worth National Bank and signed by Benton T. Lyman, Pitezel's Texas alias. In fact, Holmes had just stood at the window, crammed the cash into his pockets, retrieved a note he had already prepared, and returned to Carrie's side. The note was genuine, but it was not payable to Holmes, as he claimed, but to a businessman in Fort Worth who would never see a nickel in repayment.

He instructed Carrie to leave town immediately and visit her parents in Galva, for that was where she would be reunited with her husband. Carrie ended up with only $500 of the insurance money, and Holmes had realized about $6,500. But that wasn't enough – he also wanted Carrie's $500 and had already begun to plan how to kill the remainder of Pitezel's family.

The fall foliage was in full, brilliant color when Holmes returned to Georgiana and reported his successful business deal. He brought several gifts to mitigate her loneliness over the time he was away, and they lingered in the room, making love, until the next morning. On October 4th, Holmes accompanied his bride to the railroad station and sent her off for a visit with her parents, since he still had business to conclude in Cincinnati.

Unencumbered, Holmes set about fulfilling the rest of his malevolent plans for the Pitezel family.

Now began the odyssey across several states which would wander into Canada before finally ending in Boston following the murders of Howard, Alice, and Nettie Pitezel.

After a delightful afternoon with their "Uncle Harry," the children were happy and rambunctious upon their return to the Circle House, but when faced once again with being abandoned in the confining rented room, Howard threw a colossal hissy fit. To assuage the situation, and to eliminate future spectacles which would be remembered by witnesses, Holmes decided to isolate Howard from his sisters. He told the girls that they should wait in the hotel room for their mother,

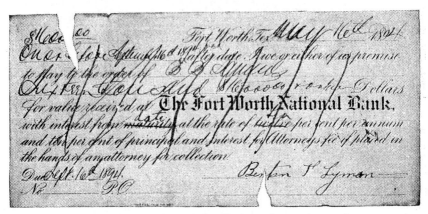

**The phony note with which Holmes claimed
Carrie Pitezel's insurance payoff.
(*The Holmes-Pitezel Case*; Frank Geyer;
Philadelphia: Publisher's Union, 1896)**

Dessie, and Wharton while he situated Howard with his friend, Minnie Williams.

The next day, when he showed up to collect Howard, the girls informed Holmes that the boy had run away. Furious, Holmes told the girls to inform Howard that "Uncle Harry" would be around to fetch him tomorrow, and he had better be ready and waiting.

Much to his misfortune, Howard complied. All three children burst into tears, clinging to one another, when Holmes came to take the boy. He soothed their grief by telling them they would all soon be united with Ben, Carrie, and their other siblings. Just be patient, he said.

In Irvington, Indiana, Holmes rented a small house that was much more secluded than the one he had abandoned in Cincinnati. Having had his scalpels, knives, and saws sharpened to razor's edges, Holmes now secured a few sticks of furniture to allay suspicions such as those that might have accompanied his actions in Cincinnati. A coal-burning stove was delivered to the little house, as well. That night, after strangling Howard, Holmes dismembered and fed the boy's body to the stove's blaze.

The very next morning, Wednesday, October 10th, he walked away from the house in Irvington and left Howard's coat with a local grocer "in hopes it would be returned to its owner." He needed to depart immediately, he said, and the boy would be by to get the coat the next day.

But young Howard would never again cross a merchant's threshold.

Soon after, Georgiana received the long-awaited telegram from her husband, telling her to meet him in Detroit. Holmes set about the same circuitous moves and hotel switches in Detroit that he had done in previous cities. Holmes surely must have possessed a brilliant mind, for the logistics of his traipse across the country were staggering. He managed to keep the three groups he was shuffling around each city – Georgiana;

The cottage in Irvington, Indiana, where
Holmes killed Howard Pitezel.
(*The Holmes-Pitezel Case*; Frank Geyer;
Philadelphia: Publisher's Union, 1896)

**No. 16 St. Vincent St., Toronoto, where Holmes
killed Nettie and Alice Pitezel.
(*The Holmes-Pitezel Case*; Frank Geyer;
Philadelphia: Publisher's Union, 1896)**

Carrie and her two wards; and Alice and Nettie – completely ignorant of each other's proximity as he moved them from place to place within a city and planned their travels.

Holmes was pondering exactly how to go about murdering Alice and Nettie. Eventually, all three of his little bands of travelers arrived in Toronto where he again ensconced them in separate hotels before going out to acquire a house in which to do his killing. The place he secured was on St. Vincent Street, and he had a few sticks of furniture delivered that afternoon along with the Pitezel girls' trunk. Alice and Nettie preceded Holmes into the little cottage, but they would never leave under their own power.

Holmes then returned to the hotel to fetch his wife, delighting her with the news of a honeymoon trip to Niagara Falls, which would precede a tour of Germany.

"I knew [Pitezel] had a family who would later afford me additional victims for the gratification of my blood-thirstiness...."

H. H. Holmes

Chapter Nine

The Homecoming

With the Pitezel girls out of the way, Holmes hurried back to the Palmer House. He and Georgiana bustled about, preparing to depart Toronto the following morning. Holmes took time out to visit Carrie Pitezel and instruct her to travel to Ogdensburg, New York, where he again promised she would be reunited with her family. In *Holmes Own Story*, trying to explain Alice and Nettie's fate, as well as that of the missing trunk, he stated:

> "I immediately returned to the Palmer House, telling my wife
> we should leave the city next morning, and said to her that if she
> had any more purchases to make, she should attend to it at once,
> as certain of the stores closed early. For the next hour I was busy
> collecting my various purchases about the city, and taking them to
> the depot to place in the large trunk, and at no later than 6:30

Hatch [this name now began to crop up in Holmes' ramblings quite frequently, but was later determined to be another of his aliases] was again at the depot, and stated that the conductor had taken the children in charge before he [Hatch] left the train. He then left me, agreeing to meet me early next morning at the hotel to learn if the children arrived all right. I then returned to the Palmer House and ate dinner.

"Without delay I went to Mrs. Pitezel's hotel, and assisted her in packing her trunk and having it taken to the train before 8 o'clock, the larger trunk going upon the same train; but Mrs. Pitezel and Dessie remarked to me later that they saw that trunk upon their arrival at Prescott early next morning, and a day later at the custom's officer at Ogdensburg, during his inspection, came across the shovel Hatch had insisted in placing in it at Detroit, remarking that he did not know but that it was dutiable on account of being new.

"If this trunk had been at the Vincent street house there would have been no necessity of one's going to the neighbors to borrow a spade with which to conceal the evidence of the terrible crime committed there. I returned to the Palmer House...and only left the hotel before taking the train next morning at 8 o'clock, for about two minutes, to step across the street and ascertain if the girls had met Miss Williams...[I was not] absent from my hotel any evening or night, save when accompanied by my wife to some place of

amusement, nor did I ever leave my hotel before 8:30 A.M., save upon this last morning.

"Thus it will be seen that this is not an unimportant statement for accounting [sic] to a witness named Rodgers, if his testimony at the inquest at Toronto is correctly reported, he saw the two children at 1 P.M. Thursday, and that early next morning a spade that had been previously borrowed had been returned to him. Again, Mr. Rodgers states that '...I fully believe that the children met their death and were buried during the night. Thursday, October 25th; the spade returned before 8 o'clock [and] that during the day their clothes were slowly burned.' ...And this while I was journeying towards Prescott, Canada, a railroad trip of about eight hours, and where I registered at the Imperial Hotel not later than 4:30 P.M. that day."

Unaware of the constant surveillance of the Pinkertons and relieved to put distance between himself and his most recent murders, Holmes hopped a train out of Toronto and continued his circuitous route toward Boston. He had already decided that abandoning his native country was imperative if he were to remain free. If he stayed in America or Canada, he would be looking over his shoulder for the rest of his life.

With a perplexed Georgiana in tow, as a blinding snow storm raged outside, Holmes left the train one stop early and hired a carriage to take them to the ferry in Ontario. Huddled together for warmth as the icy snowflakes stung their faces, Holmes must have done some fancy talking to explain leaving the warmth and safety of the railroad car for a carriage on the treacherously icy roads.

Chilled to the bone, the newlyweds were dropped at the ferry landing and crossed the choppy St. Lawrence River to Ogdensburg, New York, on Saturday, October 25, 1894. The next day Carrie, Dessie, and Wharton arrived in Ogdensburg and took a room at the National Hotel. Holmes soon arrived, telling Carrie he would leave on Tuesday for Burlington, Vermont, but she and the children should wait until November 1st, an additional three days, to follow. Ben would be in Burlington to greet her at the station.

In fact, Holmes and Georgiana arrived in Burlington on October 30th. However, he again insisted on disembarking at the preceding stop and hiring a carriage to take them the remainder of the trip. After another cold, miserable carriage ride, they were grateful for the warmth and hospitality of the Burlington Hotel. Given what had transpired since they were married, surely Georgiana suspected that all was not as it seemed. But, far from home and without funds of her own, she really had no other option but to stay with Holmes.

The next day Holmes moved them to Ahern's boardinghouse where he registered as "Mr. Hall and Wife." That afternoon, under the alias of J. A. Judson, Holmes rented a small furnished house at 26 Winoosky Avenue. He told the landlord that the rental was for his widowed sister, a Mrs. Cook.

Holmes managed to soothe Carrie's impatience after settling the three surviving Pitezels (Carrie, Dessie, and Wharton) in the little rental house and promising to leave the next morning to fetch Ben from Montreal. That evening, he told Georgiana it was necessary he take a brief business trip on behalf of his ABC Copier Company, but he would meet her in Lowell, Massachusetts in one week. From there, to fulfill his promise of a honeymoon, they would travel to Boston and board a steamship for Europe.

In fact, Dr. Holmes, nee Herman W. Mudgett, was headed to Gilmanton, New Hampshire, for a long overdue visit home.

"My pen cannot adequately portray the meeting with my aged parents, nor were it possible, would I allow it to do so for publication. Suffice it to say that I came to them as one from the dead, they for years having considered me as such, until I had written them a few days before.

"That after embracing them as I looked into their dear faces once more, my eyes grew dim with the tears kindly sent to shut out for the moment the signs of added years I knew my uncalled-for silence of the past seven years had done much to unnecessarily increase.

"For the next two days I tried to feel that I was a boy again, and when I could go away by myself for a few minutes, I would wander from room to room, taking up or passing my hands lovingly over each familiar object, opening each cupboard and drawer with the same freedom I would have used twenty years before.

"Here I found some letters written to my mother when I was a boy, and later as a young man; then as a physician, giving her careful directions regarding her health; then the letter written the day before my supposed death all bearing evidence to the many times she had sorrowfully read them. There also I found toys that years before had seemed so precious to me, and old garments carefully laid away, principally those which I had worn, and which I felt sure mother had purposely caused to be placed separately, thinking me dead, for if such had been the case it would have been the first death in our family.

"And, moreover, I had always been looked upon by the others as "mother's boy." When I went to the room where, times without number, I had been given such faithful teachings, and prayed with so earnestly, and had I been the earnest Christian my mother had then entreated me to become, I could have prayed for guidance beside the same dear old chair in which she had so often sat with me. I could not stay here. I felt it was too sacred a place to be entered now, and with tears in my eyes, that come again as I write, I reluctantly closed the door and went away."

Levi and Theodate were, indeed, overjoyed to see their son alive and well. As occasioned by the return of the Prodigal Son in the Bible, there was much celebration and joy. Then came the time for Holmes to venture to Tilton and see his wife, Clara, and their now thirteen-year-old son, Robert Lovering Mudgett. Clara swore she had never doubted that Herman would one day return and was jubilant at her husband's homecoming.

Regrettably, he said to Clara, he had a very distasteful confession to make. He told her that, mortified as he was to admit it, he had *accidentally* married another woman. Holmes claimed that after leaving Gilmanton in 1883, medical degree in hand, he had been involved in a train wreck out West and critically injured. Before being removed from the wreckage, he claimed to have been robbed of a gold watch and considerable cash. When he regained consciousness, he had no recollection of his name, no recall of his life before that very minute.

"Who I was, my name, occupation, home, parents, friends – the memory of all had fled," he said in his memoirs. "On the night of the accident, a curtain had dropped between myself and the past, and all knowledge of my former self had been swept into oblivion."

The hospital, he claimed, gave him the name of H. H. Holmes. While in this netherworld of lost identity, he was visited by a beautiful and wealthy woman who often brought gifts and read to the patients in an effort to cheer the hospital's unfortunate populace. Her name was Georgiana Yoke, and, unaware of his existing family in Gilmanton, he had fallen completely in love with her. When he was sufficiently recovered, they were married.

Unable to bear her husband's valiant, but fruitless, struggles to reclaim his memory, Georgiana hired the services of a renowned surgeon who performed a "wonderful operation" on his brain.

Upon awakening from the surgery, Holmes stated his memory had returned in a rush, but his joy rapidly turned to dismay when he realized the horrible wrong he had done to Georgiana. The kindness of that good woman, who had only ministered to him when he lay sick and helpless, had been repaid by betrayal – no matter how unwitting – on his part.

Clara apparently accepted the entire story as truth.

Holmes told his wife he would have to depart soon on an urgent business trip, but following that necessary journey, he would come back to Tilton to stay.

Never mentioning the outrageous lies he fed his family, Holmes summed up his visit to Gilmanton in his memoirs by saying,

"Later, I visited what had been my own room, finding it much as I had left it twenty years before. Many of my old school books were here, but my most precious though worthless possessions I had carefully placed elsewhere, and now I took them, dust laden, from their places of concealment. First, a complicated contrivance that when finished was to have solved the problem of perpetual motion, then a piece of a wind-mill so arranged as to make a noise when in operation sufficient to scare the crows from the corn field; going further I came to some small boxes containing almost everything from a tooth, the first I remember of having extracted, to a small bunch of very tenderly worded notes and a picture of my little twelve year old sweetheart. These experiences were repeated next day when I

drove to the old farm my grandfather had owned during his lifetime. Here mother had lived as a child, a girl, and a young woman, and accompanying me she no doubt saw many things as dear to her. I, too, had lived here for a time, and could not leave the place until I had found my 'marks' denoting my height at various times – the first of which was less than three feet.

"...Returning, I found my brother had come in answer to my request that he should visit me. He was accompanied by several sturdy boys whom I had never seen, and in whose faces I could see my brother and myself of years ago; but when, in conversation, they spoke to and of their father as 'Arthur,' his given name, I could but wonder if he thought of what would have been our portion had we ever addressed our parents in like manner...

"The next day, after a leave-taking nearly as pathetic and hard to bear as my meeting had been, I left them. I have seen neither of them since, nor do I ever expect to do so. Each prison mail delivery I receive with trembling hands, expecting it to be an announcement of their death, caused by their great sorrow and shame so cruelly forced upon them."

While Holmes was in Tilton visiting Clara and Robert, his sister had taken it upon herself to locate his "new" wife. One can only imagine the resulting conversation when the sister innocently mentioned her brother's unfortunate accident and bigamous remarriage.

After the sister-in-law left, a very confused, and surely very angry, Georgiana settled in to await her husband's return. The challenge of restoring himself to his "wife's" good graces surely required Holmes to dredge up one of his best dramatic performances.

"Our idols once shattered, though cherishing the broken
fragments as best we may, can never be the same."

Georgiana Yoke Howard

(Disillusioned wife of Holmes)

Chapter Ten

The Journey Ends

Holmes returned to Burlington and to the arms of his extremely
confused wife. Whatever he said to smooth over his sister's revelation to
Georgiana during his absence is lost to history, but it apparently worked.
After spending that day and night with his distraught "wife," Holmes
headed for the post office the next morning. While collecting his mail
he noticed he was the focus of the postal employees' attention.

*"The morning following my return to Burlington I visited the
post-office and received my mail. It had been handed to me and
I had stepped to a small desk to open some of it when, glancing toward the delivery window, I saw what seemed to me to be the entire
office force staring with all wonder at me. I knew instantly that I
was in danger, and this was made more sure to me by the manner*

in which they at once sought to dispel this feeling by dispersing from the window. I at once resumed my reading, for I felt that it would be hazardous to have them know I was aware of their acts."

Holmes pretended nonchalance, gathered his mail, and hurried back to the boarding house. With Georgiana by his side, he arrived in Boston on the evening of November 13th and checked into the Parker House. The next day, after moving to a nearby boarding house, Holmes became aware that he was again under surveillance.

No. 26 Winooski Ave., Burlington, VT, where Holmes had planned to kill the rest of Ben Pitezel's family. (*The Holmes-Pitezel Case;* Frank Geyer; Philadelphia: Publisher's Union)

He sat down and wrote a letter to Carrie instructing her to meet him in Lowell in one week. He told her to go to the basement of the Winooski Avenue house in which she was living and retrieve a bottle of expensive chemicals from behind the coal bin. She was to take the bottle to the attic

The Rogue's Gallery sketch of H. H. Holmes.

(*The Philadelphia Inquirer;* June 1895; Courtesy of the Free Library of Philadelphia)

and hide it until Holmes could fetch it. What the bottle contained was, in fact, nitroglycerine. The intention on Holmes' part was, while moving the unstable liquid about, a resulting explosion would wipe out the three surviving members of the Pitezel family. He immediately posted the letter and returned to his room. When Carrie received Holmes' letter, she headed down to the cellar to follow through with his instructions. But as she reached for the jar that would have sealed the fate of herself and her two surviving children, she was suddenly chilled by foreboding. Backing away, she left the jar where it sat and never returned to the basement again.

Meantime, John Cornish of the Pinkerton's Boston office, decided he could not wait any longer to make his move. Holmes was in a prime position to jump a steamship and leave the country for good. Since his arrival in Boston, Holmes had, in fact, checked at the Cunard Lines for departures to London At approximately 3 o'clock on Friday, November 16th, Holmes stepped from his boarding house and was immediately surrounded by four police officers. He surrendered without a struggle.

Holmes' version of the story follows:

Holmes' Rogue's Gallery entry.
(*The Philadelphia Inquirer;* June 1895; Courtesy
of the Free Library of Philadelphia)

"...*But that evening while writing some letters..., a careless
shadower, in his earnestness to learn [Carrie's] address, allowed me
to know that I was being watched. As in Burlington, I tried not*

to have it known that I had observed it, but from that moment I knew I was in their hands...After throwing off my followers, I sent this letter to Burlington by express, including tickets and full directions for their journey. I then returned to my rooms, intending to tell my wife of my threatened trouble and the causes that had led up to it, [but] I could not do it.

"We had been married less than a year, and during that time I had endeavored to shield her from all annoying influences, and to cause her such great unhappiness now, until I absolutely knew it was upon me, was impossible. The next day I was continually shadowed...

"I then went to a relative, living in a suburb, intending to ask him to aid me in making my escape by means of the trunk, if absolutely necessary. Here again my courage failed me, when I had visited him, lest it should involve him in some difficulty, and I returned to my room resolved to meet whatever was in store for me.

"Saturday P.M., November 17, I left the house intending to send two letters if possible. I had proceeded hardly a block when I was surrounded by four greatly excited men, two of whom said, 'We want you, and you are under arrest, and it will be useless for your to try to escape, as there are four of us.' I said, 'I shall make no effort to escape.' We were near the police headquarters, where I was at once taken into Inspector Watts' private office. I knew that no time would be lost in sending to my room to search my belongings, and I therefore asked that my wife be called to me, preferring to tell

her myself of what was in store for her. The request was granted, and in a few minutes she was ushered into the room.

"Of this scene I also cannot write. No one was present save Inspector Watts and I can never forget or fail to appreciate his efforts to make it as easy for her – for us both, for that matter – as was possible. Before she had left me I told her what had brought about my arrest and also my right name. Only true-hearted, loving wives, who have been made to suffer in the same way, can know what the blow meant to her. They also alone can understand her feeling expressed to me in a letter months afterwards, from which, sacred though it is to me, I quote these words, 'Our idols once shattered, though cherishing the broken fragments as best we may, can never be the same.'

"I found I had been arrested upon the charge of stealing horses in Texas, that I was to be held upon this charge until requisition and other papers could be obtained from Pennsylvania in order to have me tried in that State upon the charge of conspiring to defraud the Insurance Company in Philadelphia. I at once waived the necessity of requisition papers, and told them I was ready to go with them."

Holmes also at once confessed to the fraud in hope of being tried on that charge in Philadelphia rather than face hanging for horse theft in Texas. Holmes memoirs state,

"I was then closely questioned regarding the whereabouts of the Pitezel family, and knowing that Mrs. Pitezel would in a few days be in Lowell with no one to plan and care for her, I thought it best to tell them where she was, asking them to meet her upon her

arrival...In my interview with Mr. Perry, the company's representative, it was agreed that in consideration of my aiding them in clearing up the case, that I could depend upon the company's influence and aid in selecting a suitable location for a home for my wife in Philadelphia. That my name, then only known to a few persons, should be withheld, allowing me to appear before the public as H. H. Holmes, thus shielding my relatives from disgrace."

Carrie Pitezel also gave no resistance to arrest. On November 19th, 1894, Thomas G. Crawford of the Philadelphia police arrived to take Holmes and Carrie into custody. Both prisoners agreed to accompany Crawford to Pennsylvania without the formality of extradition.

During the train ride back to Philadelphia, Holmes joked good naturedly about how badly Pitezel had bungled the fraud setup. He also bragged about his ability to hypnotize people and offered the detective $500 if Crawford would allow himself to be hypnotized. Crawford declined, giving the droll excuse that hypnosis tended to spoil his appetite and cause him indigestion.

The train arrived in Philadelphia the next day. Carrie Pitezel and Holmes were immediately taken to city hall for questioning. A brief hearing determined that the two would await trial in Moyamensing Prison. Dessie and baby Wharton were given over to Benjamin Crew of the Society to Protect Children from Cruelty. Within days Jeptha Howe was brought from St. Louis and held on $2,500 bail.

District Attorney George S. Graham then indicted the three, along with Benjamin Pitezel, for conspiring to cheat and defraud the Fidelity Mutual Life Association.

"Like the man eating tiger of the tropical jungle, whose
appetite for blood has once been aroused, I roamed
about the world seeking whom I could destroy."

H. H. Holmes

Chapter Eleven

Enter Frank Geyer

A twenty-year veteran of the Philadelphia Police Department's detective unit, Frank P. Geyer was a beefy, balding man with thick slanted
eyebrows and a bushy mustache. Considered the best detective in the
department, Geyer had apprehended a number of burglars, conmen,
gangsters, and murderers during his stellar career. The murder case
that haunted him most was that of Annie Gaskins, a woman who slit
her baby's throat and then claimed that her cat had attacked the infant.
Because of his past successes, Geyer was assigned to Holmes' case.

"About the time of the trial and conviction of Holmes,"
Geyer stated later in his book, *The Holmes-Pitezel Case*, "I
was sent for by Mr. Barlow, to call upon him at the District
Attorney's office. On my arrival there, I was informed that Mr.

Frank Geyer, Philadelphia Police Detective
(*The Holmes-Pitezel Case*; Frank Geyer;
Philadelphia: Publisher's Union, 1896)

Graham had decided to send me West to make a search for the missing Pitezel children. Arrangements were then made with the superintendent of police to detail me for the task...Eight months having elapsed since the children had been heard from, it did not look like a very encouraging task to undertake, and it was the general belief of all interested, that the children would never be found. The District Attorney believed, however, that another final effort to find the children should be made, for the sake of the stricken mother, if for nothing else."

At the time of Barlow's request, Geyer was still in deep mourning over the loss of his wife, Martha, and their twelve-year-old daughter,

Esther, in a house fire only three months earlier. Geyer's personal opinion was that no horror could compare to the death of a child, and the thought that one human purposely inflicted that agony on another was intolerable. He was determined to locate the children's bodies, both to bring peace to the bereft Carrie Pitezel and justice for the children. He would use the youngsters' unposted letters found in Holmes' possession, for the children had dated each one and marked the city from which they were written. These were the only leads Geyer had to recreate Holmes' circuitous trek across North America.

Geyer left Philadelphia on Wednesday evening, June 26th, 1895, and arrived in Cincinnati on the 27th at 7:30. The detective registered at the Palace Hotel before heading to the police department to meet with his old friend, Detective John Shnooks. The two friends talked of shared cases and old times before Geyer retired to the hotel for a good night's sleep.

The next morning, Geyer presented the reason for his visit to Superintendent Philip Dietsch, who instructed Shnooks to assist the visiting detective in any and all ways possible. In Geyer's own words, he left with Shnooks and,

> "...commenced the greatest search I have ever had in my twenty years' experience in the detective business...[in my possession] were photographs of Holmes, Pitezel, Alice, Nettie, and Howard Pitezel, Mrs. Pitezel, Dessie and the baby, also of Mrs. Pitezel's trunk...a photograph of a missing trunk which be-

longed to the children; also a trunk belonging to Mrs. Howard [Georgiana].

Armed with these photos, Geyer and Shnooks began to systematically visit every hotel near the train depots. After several failures, they found an entry of interest on the registry of the Atlantic House. The record for Friday, September 28th, 1894, included the name Alex E. Cook, with three children. The best the clerk could do was to say the photos resembled the foursome, who had stayed only the one night. At the Hotel Bristol, however, A. E. Cook and three children had spent the night of September 29th. This time, however, clerk W. L. Bain recognized the pictures Geyer showed him. But the little "family" had checked out the next morning.

"Knowing that Holmes was in the habit of renting houses in most every city he visited, I determined to give up the search among the hotels and make some inquiry among the real estate agents...After visiting quite a number of them, we called at the office of J. C. Thomas. We showed him the pictures of Holmes and Howard Pitezel, which he immediately recognized as that of a man who had a small boy with him, and who rented a house from him at No. 305 Poplar Street, on Friday, September 28th, 1894, paying $15 in advance for it and giving the name of A. C. Hayes."

Thomas told Geyer and Shnooks that his tenant had only stayed in the house a couple of days before leaving without word. He suggested the detectives interview a Miss Hill, who lived next door to the rented house.

"[Miss Hill] said there was really very little to tell. The first she noticed of [Holmes] was on Saturday morning...when a furniture wagon was driven in front of No. 305...and a man and small boy alighted. The man took a key out of his pocket, and after opening the door of No. 305, a large, iron cylinder stove...was taken out of the wagon and carried into the house. She was doubtless observed by Holmes...for on the next morning, September 30th, (Sunday) he rang her bell, and told her he was not going to occupy the house and that she could have the stove.

"I was not able to appreciate the intense significance of the renting of the Poplar Street house and the delivery of a stove of such immense size there, but I felt sure I was on the right track and so started for Indianapolis, from which point several of the children's letters found in Holmes' tin box had been dated."

From Cincinnati, Geyer traveled to Indianapolis, arriving on June 29th. He registered at the Spencer House and then made his way to police headquarters on Alabama Street. Detective David Richards was assigned to assist Geyer, and they began a canvass of the hotels near Union Depot.

"Going to the Stubbins House and examining the register, we found that on September 24th, 1894, was an entry in the name of Etta Pitsel, St. Louis, Mo.,and...she left on the morning

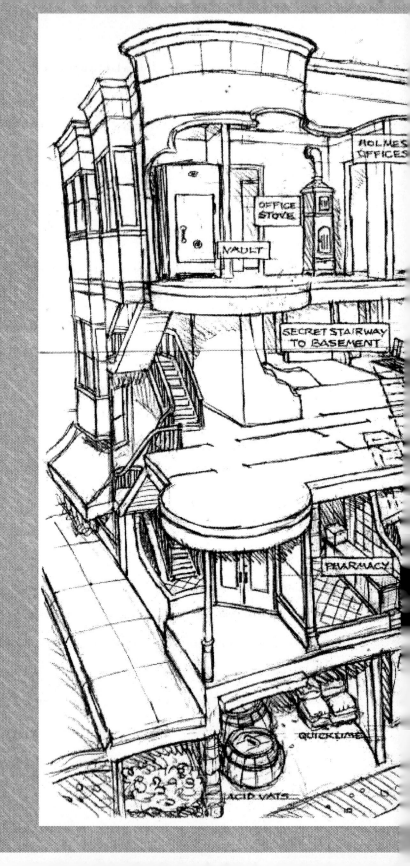

SHAFT FROM ROOF TO BASEMENT

AUTOPSY TABLE

ELASTICITY DETERMINATOR

ATORY

(Cutaway sketch by Rick Geary, author and illustrator of *The Beast of Chicago: An Account of the Life and Crimes of Herman W. Mudgett, Known to the World as H. H. Holmes.* www.rickgeary.com)

of September 28th. Further inquiry elicited the fact that the girl was brought there by a man known to Mr. Robert Sweeney, the clerk, as Mr. Howard, and that on Friday morning, September 28th, he had received a telegram from Mr. Howard, dated St. Louis, requesting him to have Etta Pitsel [sic] at the Union Depot to meet the St. Louis train [which Howard would be on] for Cincinnati, Ohio. [This was the day Holmes left St. Louis with Nettie and Howard Pitezel, telling their mother that he was going to take them to Indianapolis, where they would be taken care of by a kind old lady.]

"We then went to the place known as the Circle, where there are several hotels."

At the Hotel English, Geyer found an entry for the three "Canning" children of Galva, Illinois, on September 30th. He showed the hotel clerk photos of the Pitezel children, and the clerk identified them as the "Canning" youngsters, and also recognized Holmes' picture as the man accompanying them. The foursome left the next morning, October 1st.

"Knowing that the children's grandparents' name was Canning and that they lived in Galva, Illinois, I was convinced that I was on the right track, and with renewed energy, I determined to find out where they were taken to on Monday morning, October 1st. Every hotel and lodging house in Indianapolis was searched, but no record could be found of where the children had stopped."

May 29. 95

Dist Attorney Graham
      Dear Sir :-
The adv. should appear in the N.Y. Sunday Herald
+ if some comment upon the case can also be put in
body of paper stating absence of children + that
adv concerning appears in this paper etc it would
be an advantage - Any words you may see fit
to use in adv. will do + if a long one only one
sentence need be in cipher as she will know
by this that it must come from me or no one else
unless I told them, hes Sam &
Perhaps the 1st-sentence should be "Important
to her before 10th, Cable. Also write to Mrs Massie
A & L b c a R u n - n b - C B R c - etc
The N Y Herald is (or was a year ago) to be found
at only a few places regularly in London x.
      Very Respectfully
            H.H.Holmes

REPUBLICAN republican uvwxyz. Thus ClepBc
ABCDEFGHIJ klmnopqrst   Holmes

**Desperately trying to prove that the Pitezel children were alive
and well and traveling with Minnie Williams in Europe, Holmes
wrote this letter to D. A. Graham explaining the "Republican
Code." Holmes claimed that he and Minnie had agreed to use
in order to communicate while she was abroad. Along with
the letter, Holmes submitted a message (written in the code) to
be run in the *New York Times* personal ads. This, he said, was
the newspaper Minnie would be watching for messages from
him (Holmes). There was, of course, no response to the ad.**

**(*The Philadelphia Inquirer,* October 1895; courtesy
of the Free Library of Philadelphia)**

It eventually dawned on Richards there had been a hotel within
fifty feet of the Circle Hotel, called the Circle House, that had gone
out of business since September, 1894. Though the former proprietor

of the inn did not live nearby, the man who had been his clerk, a man named Reisner, worked near the Union depot. He met the detectives the next morning at the office of the attorney who now had the Circle House Hotel's records. In the register, on October 1st, 1894, were the three Canning children of Galva, Illinois. Though the hotel's records had been haphazardly kept, Reisner told the detectives that the Canning party had stayed until October 6th. Geyer also found Georgiana registered at the Circle Park Hotel from September 18th through the 24th. She would register again on the 30th and stay until October 4th. That was the period during which Holmes and Alice Pitezel were in Philadelphia to identify Pitezel's body. Geyer would later comment in his book,

"While at the Circle Park Hotel, Mrs. Howard became very intimate with the proprietress, a Mrs. Rodius. She informed [Rodius] that her husband was a very wealthy man, and that he owned real estate and cattle ranches in Texas; also had considerable real estate in Berlin, Germany, where they intended to go as soon as her husband could get his business affairs into shape to leave."

The Circle Park Hotel where Georgiana stayed was less than 100 feet from the Circle House where the Pitezel children were staying.

Geyer then decided to interview the defunct Circle House Hotel's former proprietor, a man named Ackelow, who now lived in West Indianapolis. Ackelow had a vivid recollection of the three Pitezel children and their "uncle, Mr. Howard." Holmes said that the children's mother, his sister, had been recently widowed and would soon join them.

"[Holmes] said that Howard was a very bad boy and that he was trying to place him in some institution, or bind him out to some farmer, as he wanted to get rid of the responsibility of looking after him.

"[Ackelow also said] that on numerous occasions he had sent his oldest boy up to the children's room to call them for their meals. His son would return to him and tell him that he found the children crying, --evidently heartbroken and home-sick to see their mother, or hear from her."

Holmes' comment about Howard being "a very bad boy" convinced Geyer even more that the child had been killed, but he had no idea where. Although he was certain that Howard had not left Indianapolis alive, Geyer abandoned the search there for the time being and traveled on to Chicago. Outside of having been Holmes' residence for several years, Geyer learned the chambermaid who had charge of the children's room at the Circle House, Caroline Klausmann, had relocated to Chicago. When Geyer showed Klausmann the photos, her eyes filled with tears.

"She said that the children were always drawing pictures of houses, or engaged in writing, and that she frequently went into their room and found them crying. Observing that they were alone at the hotel, she naturally believed they were orphan children...crying over the loss of their father and mother."

Throughout his various confessions or during his interviews with the authorities, Holmes continually spoke of a man named Edward

Hatch. According to Holmes, Hatch was responsible for just about all of the evil activities attributed to him (Holmes). It was Hatch, a bricklayer who had done odd jobs around the Castle for Holmes, who had the children. When Geyer told Pat Quinlan that Holmes was now claiming that the children were in Hatch's care, Quinlan denounced Holmes as a "dirty, lying scoundrel" and stated Hatch would never do anything wrong. Eventually, the name Edward Hatch would be added to Holmes' long list of aliases.

Geyer now traveled to Detroit where he found several people who recognized Alice and Nettie, as well as Carrie Pitezel, Dessie, and baby Wharton. Cruelly, Carrie was often within just a few blocks of her missing children's hotel room. She, however, was never aware of their

```
                                    Chicago, Aug. 2nd. '95

Friend H.H.H.

        I, and Jim, will not, saw and, split, the wood. They, can't and,
don't, want to, know, whether there is, anything, around or, about, the, con-
servatory or, green-nouse.,      I, think, will leave, the dog, for, Mrs. John,
Cleveland, at Bleak House, tomorrow. Will, join him under, cover, and fix,
all, circus board, signs, there. Same, time I will, sighfor, Ponto's fate
and yours in his misfortune.

                                Friend,

                                L.S. Page.
```

R.I.T.U.A.L.

When the ad written in the "Republican Code" drew no response, Holmes revealed a second code he and Minnie used based on the word "RITUAL." Holmes submitted the above ad, in the "RITUAL" code to be published in the New York Times. There was no response to this ad, either.
(*The Philadelphia Inquirer;* April 12, 1896; Courtesy of the Free Library of Philadelphia)

**The grave of Alice and Nettie Pitezel in the
basement of the Toronto House.**

**(*The Philadelphia Inquirer;* July 1895; Courtesy
of the Free Library of Philadelphia)**

proximity. Geyer visited every hotel and rooming house, and actually
found a couple of people who recognized Howard's photo, destroying
his theory the boy was killed in Indianapolis. At this point in Geyer's
book, the reader becomes aware of a grudging admiration for Holmes'
intelligence, nimble mind, and unflagging charm.

"It must have taken very careful management to have moved
these three separate parties [Nettie, Alice, and Howard; Carrie,
Dessie and the baby; and Georgiana] from Detroit to Toronto,

without either of the three discovering either of the others, but this great expert in crime did it, and did it successfully."

Geyer now moved on to Toronto, a city to which he was not a stranger. An old friend, Detective Alf Cuddy, was assigned to assist the Philadelphia cop with his search. In their canvass of the hotels, seeking entries for October 19th, they found "G. Howell and wife" registered at the Walker House, Mrs. C. A. Adams and daughter at the Union House, and Alice and Nettie Canning were registered at the Albion. Holmes left the Walker House on the afternoon of October 20th.

But Geyer knew the man was in Toronto as late as October 25th. He also was aware that, in addition to hotel rooms, Holmes had rented at least one small house in each of the cities in which they stopped.

"So thoroughly convinced was I that Holmes had rented a house in Toronto, Ontario, that...I wrote in my report to the Superintendent of Police in Philadelphia, dated at Toronto, July 9th, 1895, the following:

"It is my impression that Holmes rented a house in Toronto the same as he did in Cincinnati...and Detroit...and that on the 25th of October he murdered the girls and disposed of their bodies by either burying them in the cellar, or some convenient place, or burning them in the heater. I intend to go to the real estate agents and see if they can recollect having rented a house about that time to a man who only occupied it for a few days..."

Geyer took a Toronto directory and prepared to visit each and every real estate agent in the city. After he and Cuddy spent a tiring and fruitless day pounding the pavement, Geyer decided to go to the newspapers.

"I gave them the whole story, and told them I was prepared to let them have the photographs of Holmes and the children, and would esteem it a favor if they would publish them. I also requested them to call the attention of real estate agents and private renters to the matter, so that if any person had rented a house under such circumstances as I described, I would be glad to have them communicate with me. The next morning every newspaper published in Toronto, devoted several columns to the story of the disappearance of the children, and requested all good citizens to forward any information...to Police Headquarters, or to me at the Rossin House."

Except for a short sojourn to Niagara Falls, Geyer spent his days searching for real estate agents who might remember Holmes. Discouraged but determined, Geyer found an ad in the paper one morning about a house for rent at No. 16 St. Vincent Street. It happened that Detective Cuddy was acquainted with the couple who owned the place, and they hastened to the man's house with Holmes' photo.

No. 16 was a two-story cottage that stood back from the sidewalk a few feet, its tiny front yard enclosed with a wire net fence about five feet high. Flowers blossomed in the garden and a clinging clematis wound up the veranda.

The detectives didn't go directly to No. 16, but stopped at No. 18 to chat with the occupant of that house, Thomas William Ryves. Ryves identified Holmes and the Pitezel girls as having occupied No. 16 for about a week in October. Geyer wrote:

"He told us that the man asked him to loan him a spade, as he wanted to arrange a place in the cellar for his sister to put potatoes in. He said that the only furniture brought to the house was an old bed and mattress and a big trunk."

The two detectives then located the owners, No. 16 Vincent Street being occupied at that time, and secured permission to search the house. Mrs. Armbrust (the tenant) also granted them permission to search her home, and they borrowed Ryves' spade.

"She kindly consented and ushered us back into the kitchen. Lifting a large piece of oilcloth from the floor, we discovered a small trap door, possibly two feet square in about the centre of the room. Raising this, I discovered that the cellar was not very deep but it was very dark, so I asked Mrs. Armbrust to kindly provide us with some lamps. In a short time she had them ready, and down into the cellar we went. The cellar was very small, about ten feet square, and not more than four and a half feet in depth. A set of steps almost perpendicular lead to it from the old-fashioned trap door in the middle of the kitchen floor.

"Taking the spade and pushing it into the earth, so as to determine whether it had been lately dug up, we finally discovered a soft spot in the southwest corner. Forcing the spade into the earth, we found it easy digging, and after going down about one foot, a horrible stench arose. This convinced us that we were on the right spot, and our coats were thrown off, and with renewed confidence, we continued our digging.

"The deeper we dug, the more horrible the odor became, and when we reached the depth of three feet, we discovered what appeared to be the bone of the forearm of a human being."

With this discovery, Geyer abandoned the digging for the time being so an undertaker could be summoned. They returned to the Vincent Street house with B. D. Humphrey, who was charged with removing the remains. Geyer wrote:

"Mr. Humphrey after preparing himself for the task (rubber gloves, etc.), jumped into the hole already made by Cuddy and myself and assisted us in the work. In a short time we unearthed the remains of the two little girls, Alice and Nettie Pitezel.

"Alice was found lying on her side, with her hand to the west. Nettie

Holmes borrowed this spade from a neighbor to dig the girls' grave. (*The Holmes-Pitezel Case*; Frank Geyer; Philadelphia: Publisher's Union, 1896)

was found lying on her face, with her head to the south, her plaited hair hanging neatly down her back."

Humphrey then sent a messenger back to his place of business with instructions to bring two coffins. When they arrived, the coffins were brought into the kitchen.

"...we proceeded to lift the remains out of the hole. As Nettie's limbs were found resting on Alice's, we first began with her. We lifted her gently as possible, but owing to the decomposed state of the body, the weight of her plaited hair hanging down her back, pulled the scalp from off her head."

Nettie was born with a club foot, and the bottom part of the corpse's right leg had been removed by Holmes, probably to complicate identifying her, should the body be found. They placed her fragile body on a sheet and started moving it up the stairs to its coffin. The team went back down to the cellar, placed Alice's corpse on a sheet and moved it up to the kitchen, into its coffin, as well. The girls' bodies were mostly nude, with only part of a blouse and a length of ribbon found in their shallow grave.

Mrs. Armbrust told Geyer that when she moved into the house, she noticed some rags and straw hanging from the chimney in the north front room. She pulled them out and discovered a striped blouse, part of a woolen garment, and a blue dress. The straw was scorched, but the items had not burned due to the clothing being stuffed so tightly into the chimney. A pair of girl's button boots, one other boot, and parts of female clothing had been found in the wood box by Mrs. Armbrust, who had discarded the items. Geyer later wrote that every inch of the cellar, as well as the dirt floors of the barn and outhouses, were dug up, but nothing else of interest was found.

Reporters, sketch artists, and the curious besieged the little house. The bodies were moved to Mr. Humphrey's mortuary. Everyone seemed pleased with Geyer's success, but that satisfaction was mingled with the sad and horrifing fate of fifteen-year-old Alice and twelve-year-old Nettie. Geyer said,

> "...and thus it was proved that little children cannot be murdered in this day and generation, beyond the possibility of discovery."

On July 18th, at 7:30 p.m., Geyer fought his way through the throngs of reporters and curious citizens to rescue Carrie Pitezel as she stepped from the Canadian Pacific train that brought her to Toronto. He hustled the grieving mother into a waiting carriage and ensconced her in a room adjoining his at the Rossin House Hotel and requested no one disturb her.

Carrie was prostrate from grief, as well as the fatigue of making the trip to Toronto. When she was sufficiently revived, she asked Geyer if he was certain the bodies in the cellar were those of her daughters. As gently as possible, the detective affirmed Carrie's worst fears. He stayed with her only a short time and then asked several of the female staff to check on Carrie frequently while he made arrangements to take her to the morgue to identify her children. He wrote,

"Cuddy and I then returned to the hotel, where every care that human forethought could suggest, had been taken to prepare Mrs. Pitezel for the awful task necessity [sic] imposed upon her. I told her that it would be absolutely impossible for her to see anything but Alice's teeth and hair, and only the hair belonging to Nettie. This had a paralyzing effect upon her and she almost fainted. At 4 P.M. we had a carriage at the Rossin House, and I informed her that we were ready to proceed to the morgue.

"Coroner Johnston, Dr. Craven and several of his assistants, had removed the putrid flesh from the skull of Alice; the teeth had been nicely cleaned and the bodies covered with canvas. The head of Alice was covered with paper, and a hole sufficiently large had been cut in it, so that Mrs. Pitezel could see the teeth. The hair of both children had been carefully washed and laid on the canvass sheet which was covering Alice.

"With Cuddy on one side of her, and I on the other, we entered and led her up to the slab, upon which was lying all that remained of poor Alice. In an instant she recognized the teeth and hair as that of her daughter Alice. Then, turning around to me she said, 'Where is Nettie?'

"About this time she noticed the long black plait of hair belonging to Nettie lying in the canvass. She could stand it no longer, and the shrieks of that poor forlorn creature are still ringing in my ears. Tears were trickling down the cheeks of strong men who stood about us. The sufferings of the stricken mother were beyond description.

"We gently led her out of the room, and into the carriage. She returned to the Rossin House completely overcome with grief and despair, and had one fainting spell after another."

The coroner requested Carrie's presence at the inquest later that day, and at 7:30 p.m., Geyer flagged down a carriage and accompanied her to city hall. In a weak, barely audible voice, Carrie testified for two and a half hours. When she was finally allowed to leave the stand, Carrie was taken to the matron's room. She had scarcely gotten there when she became hysterical, and according to Geyer, "...her shrieks for Alice, Nettie and Howard, could have been heard a block away."

But there was still one more onerous duty to be fulfilled for Carrie – the interment of her daughters. On the afternoon of July 19, 1895, the bodies of her little girls were buried in St. James' cemetery, the expense being covered by the Toronto authorities. Following the dismal funeral, Carrie returned to Chicago while Geyer renewed his search for Howard. He still wanted to believe that Howard had been placed in an institution, as Holmes claimed, or that he was hidden in some obscure place.

Geyer's greatest hope was that somehow, some way, Howard would be found alive and well – although in his heart of hearts he knew that the boy was already dead.

In a letter written while in Detroit, Alice had stated that, "Howard is not with us now," but she didn't say exactly when they were separated.

There really was no evidence that Howard had made it to Detroit, so Geyer turned his efforts once again to Indianapolis. With the help of Detective David Richards, Geyer repeated his canvas of real estate agencies.

Geyer wrote to Philadelphia Superintendent of Police Linden that, "By Monday we will have searched every outlying town, except Irvington, and another day will conclude that. After Irvington, I scarcely know where we shall go."

A trolley delivered the two detectives to Irvington on Tuesday to resume their search. Finally, fate swung in their favor. At the very first real estate office they visited, that of a Mr. Brown, they hit pay dirt. After studying the photos and documents that Geyer had taken all over the country, he recognized Holmes as a man who had rented a house from him in October of 1894. Holmes had been quite sharp and disrespectful of Brown, which made him more memorable. The doctor who owned the little cottage also recognized Holmes' picture and one of Dr. Thompson's employees remembered Howard as well.

The two men searched the cellar first, but the ground there was unmarred by any shovel. Upon surveying the outside of the house, Geyer found a piece of trunk that he kept as evidence. Dreading the unavoidable discovery of Howard's remains, he turned his attention to the barn and outhouses.

Inside the barn, his heart stopped at the sight of a huge blood-stained coal stove over three feet tall. A soft patch of soil caught their attention and they dug deeply, but found nothing. Word of their mission had spread around the neighborhood and they now had an audience of several hundred huddled around the house. The weary detectives returned to town where Geyer sent a telegram to Carrie asking about a strip of blue calico on the trunk piece he had found. As he knew she would, Carrie confirmed that he had, indeed, located the children's missing trunk.

But while in the telegraph office, Geyer received a call from an editor at the Indianapolis *Evening News* asking him to wait there to meet with Dr. Thompson (the owner of the house) and his friend Dr. Barnhill. The two doctors had decided to continue the search after the cops left and were joined by a couple of boys, Walter Jenny and Oscar Kettenbach, who wanted to help. The boys decided to go back down to the cellar, even though Geyer had found no evidence of Howard there.

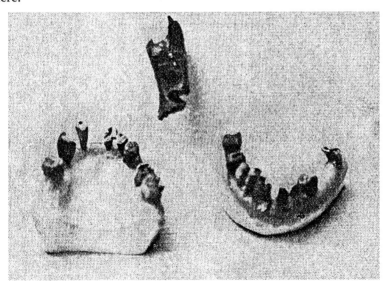

Howard Pitezel's teeth and jawbone.
(*The Holmes-Pitezel Case*; Frank Geyer;
Philadelphia: Publisher's Union, 1896)

In the basement chimney, Walter stuck his arm into the pipe's opening and was rewarded with not only a handful of ashes, but some pieces of bone, as well. Excited and breathless, the boys relayed the discovery to the adults. They had found Howard's femur.

Now the two detectives and the two doctors hurried back to the main house, where they found the whole neighborhood gathered. News of the boys' find had spread like wildfire. When the police arrived, they banned everyone but Geyer, his friend, the two medical men, and some reporters. Geyer dismantled the lower part of the chimney with a hammer and chisel, sifted the resulting material through a piece of screen he found, and was rewarded with an almost complete set of teeth and piece of Howard's jaw.

Upon searching the bottom of the chimney, they found not only the boy's pelvis, but a portion of his hard-baked stomach, liver, and spleen. Iron fastenings for the trunk were uncovered, some buttons, a pin, and a crochet needle. It wasn't long before the grocer with Howard's coat showed up, recognized Holmes picture, and made identity of the remains concrete.

Again, Geyer had the painful task of contacting Carrie Pitezel with news of the death of yet another of her children. She left her parents' home in Galva and traveled to Indiana for the coroner's inquest. Carrie identified Howard's coat, the strip of calico on the trunk, and a couple of trinkets Ben had gotten Howard at the world's fair. The scarfpin, a pair of shoes, and the crochet needle were Alice's.

"I was born with the evil one standing as my spon-

sor...and he has been with me ever since."

H. H. Holmes

Chapter Twelve

Counsel for the Defense:

Preparing for Trial

The day following the discovery of Howard's scant remains, Geyer and Gary were called before a grand jury at the county's court house. They recited the entire Holmes story to the jurors. Following that, the coroner organized an inquest to formally identify the victim whose bones had been found.

Once again, Carrie Pitezel was summoned to make the identification. Even though she knew the girls were dead, Carrie had clung to the hope that Holmes had, indeed, left Howard at a reform school as he had so often threatened. Therefore, the Irvington discovery was devastating to her.

There was no way to shield Carrie from the brutal truth of Howard's death. With his surgical instruments newly sharpened, Holmes had, after strangling the boy, sawed the arms, legs, and head off the child's body. He fed each of these smaller portions of flesh into the stove, keeping the fire going until all of Howard's remains had been incinerated. The only parts of Howard's body found, his teeth and jawbone, were not much help for identification.

The dentist, Dr. Byram, said that the teeth and jawbone were from a child between eight and eleven years old, and a Dr. Barnhill testified that the remaining bones were those of a child of seven to ten years.

∾

When the news of the children's remains reached Chicago, the authorities there decided it would be prudent to search the Castle owned

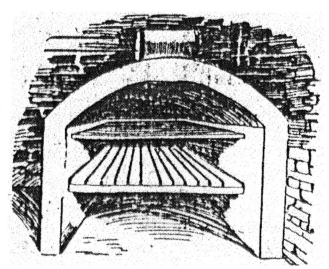

The oven in the basement of Holmes' Castle. The metal rack rolled out, making it a perfect crematory. (*Chicago Times-Herald;* July 25, 1895; Courtesy of the Abraham Lincoln Presidential Library).

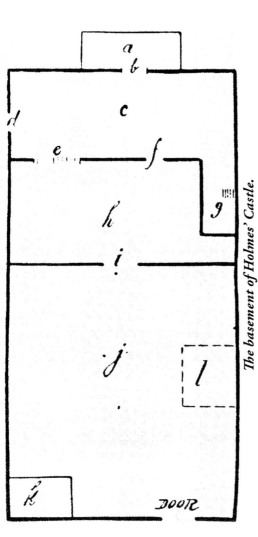

The basement of Holmes' Castle.

A – Gas tank under alleyway.

B – Entrance into the walled-off portion of the basement.

C – South end of basement.

D – Window and door under sidewalk.

E – Stairway from rear.

F – Entrance to center of basement.

G – Secret chamber, with stairway on west side, concealed by manure and dirt and opened by police; a woman's shoe was fund four feet underground.

H – Center of basement.

I – Entrance to north end of basement

J – North end of basement.

K – Coal bin underneath which a shirt and drawers were found.

L – Bottom of elevator shaft, reached by concealed stairs and a false trap door in bathroom on second floor.

(*The Chicago Times-Hearld;* July 25, 1895; Courtesy the Abraham Lincoln Presidential Library).

by the man they now believed to be a killer. Very little of the building was occupied at the time, the only tenants being a few businesses on the first floor. What the police found as they wandered through the second and third floors of the building left them quite puzzled – the sliding doors, secret stairways, and strangely constructed rooms made little sense. They found what could have been a laundry chute but for

DEPARTMENT OF BUILDINGS
Joseph Downey, Commissioner

Chicago, July 23d, 1895

Special report on H. H. Holmes' Building, S.W. Corner 63rd and Wallace streets:

Size of building, 50 x 125 feet, three-story and basement; stores and flats, five stores, two facing 63rd Street, and three on Wallace Street.

The structural parts of inside are all weak and dangerous. Built of the poorest and cheapest kind of material. A combination bay window and winding stairway on Wallace Street side, starting at second story joist and projecting three feet from building line, is breaking away from the building and is dangerous.

All dividing partitions between flats are combustible. Building was built in sections, and several parts weakened by fire, and not properly repaired. There is an uneven settlement of foundations, in some places as much as four inches in a span of 20 feet. The temporary roof put up after fire in the building is not properly constructed. The secret stairway and trap door leading from the bathroom and also underground gas tank does not interfere with the construction of the building. The stores are the only habitable parts of the building. The rest of the building should be condemned. The sanitary condition of the building is horrible.

Respectfully submitted,

E. F. LAUGHLIN,
Inspector.

**The letter from Building Inspector E. F. Laughlin
condemning the Holmes' Castle.
(Courtesy the Abraham Lincoln Presidential Library).**

The quick lime pit in the basement of the Castle.
(*Chicago Times-Herald;* July 25, 1895; Courtesy of
the Abraham Lincoln Presidential Library).

Searchers work by
electric light to recover
human remains from
the Castle's basement.
(*Chicago Times-Herald;*
July 25, 1895; Courtesy
of the Abraham Lincoln
Presidential Library).

the fact that it was coated with grease.

What they discovered in the basement, however, was both terrifying and mesmerizing. Holding a torch to light their way, they braved the overwhelming stench that blasted forth upon opening a bathroom's trap door and carefully made their way down the hidden stairway and into the bowels of Holmes' madness.

In one corner of the dank, dark area was a pile of bones... some human and others the detritus of many meals. The torch held high, they traversed the entire area, passing Holmes' "human elasticizer," his dissecting table next to the cabinet of

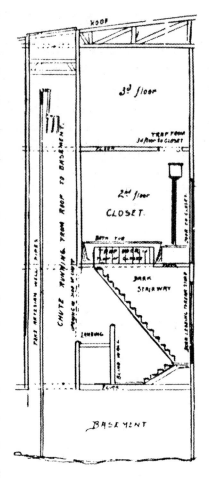

This secret staircase inside the vacant elevator shaft led from Holmes' office to the street or basement.

(*The Chicago Times*; August 1895; Courtesy of the Abraham Lincoln Presidential Library)

surgical instruments, and vats of acid. A huge quicklime pit sprouted bones stripped of flesh as well as body parts in varying stages of decomposition.

One policeman noted that the basement seemed much smaller than the spacious upper stories and began looking for another hidden portal. Finding none, the cops located a sledge and slammed it into a brick wall to create an opening through which they could access the other side. This was the wall behind which the gas machine had stood.

Apparently, gas fumes had built up behind the wall, and as soon as the first man introduced the torch to light his way into the hidden area, there was a huge explosion. The blast sent several of the men tumbling across the muck of the floor. A few required medical attention, but their determined colleagues continued their trek into the walled-off room.

When the search of the Castle was finally finished, authorities concluded that there was evidence of as many as two hundred people killed in Holmes' murder factory. Human remains were found not only in the basement, but in fireplaces, chimneys, and stoves throughout the structure. Combine those findings with corpses vaporized in the crematory, sold to medical schools, dumped elsewhere, or rearticulated as skeletons...not to mention murders committed outside of Chicago... and the number of lives claimed by the killer is difficult to even contemplate.

All that is certain is that Holmes was appallingly adept at satisfying his appetite for blood.

"I could not help the fact that I was a murderer, no
more than the poet can help the inspiration to song, nor
the ambition of an intellectual man to be great."

H. H. Holmes

Chapter Thirteen

A Jury of His Peers

The chill of late fall embraced Philadelphia's hulking gray City
Hall on Monday, October 28, 1895 – the first day of Holmes' trial.
Inside the courtroom, the 500-seat spectator's gallery was empty as The
Honorable Michael Arnold climbed up to take his place behind the
huge marble desk that was his bench. The public would be allowed in
once testimony began. Holmes' attorneys, as well as District Attorney
George Graham and his assistant, were already seated at their respec-
tive tables.

On one side of the courtroom was a tunnel of steel bars – a sort of
cage built along that wall. This was the path from the holding cell to
the courtroom. Holmes came through the tunnel, walking lightly on
his toes.

"Put Herman W. Mudgett, alias H. H. Holmes, in the dock," came the order from the court clerk.

Holmes now bore little resemblance to the jaunty fellow who had arrived in Philadelphia a few months earlier. Pale and thin, he had grown a pointed black beard that now disguised his sallow face. The black double-breasted suit he wore, once tailored to fit perfectly, hung loosely about his shoulders and his collar sagged.

The New York World described him as follows: "A thin, wasted man, weighing perhaps 120 pounds; a man with a keen but intensely repulsive face; a face shaped like a hatchet...The remarkable feature is the nose. It is such a nose as hangmen rarely meet in their business capacity. It is well developed, beautifully chiseled, a Greek nose of the finest pattern...The shape of the head is unusual, abnormal. The forehead is fairly good, except that it lacks development at the top...There is in the face nothing to explain the singular power this man has to win the love and confidence of women whom he betrayed and murdered.

"The upper lip seems to extend beyond the lower, and every few seconds he rubs the knuckles of one hand against the fingers of the other...The skull [is] so abnormally shaped at the back; but it is not so abnormal as the murderer's ear. That was as small as a little girl's, twisted out of shape so that the inner part sticks out beyond the outer rim...It is a marvelously small ear, and at the top it is shaped and carved after the fashion in which old sculptors indicated deviltry [sic] and vice in their statues of satyrs...The tophead [sic] is flat, except for one sharp

Holmes is arraigned in Philadelphia.
(***Philadelphia Public Ledger;*** **Sept. 24, 1895;**
Courtesy the Free Library of Philadelphia).

bump rising suddenly and sharply. The eyes are very big and wide open. They are blue."

The reporter then makes this astounding statement: "Great murderers, like great men in other walks of activity, have blue eyes."

Holmes strode to the prisoner's dock and sat down.

He was ordered to stand, at which time his counsel, William A. Shoemaker and Samuel P. Rotan, joined him, to hear the bill of indictment charging Holmes with the murder of Benjamin F. Pitezel. Though his fingers fidgeted where they grasped the rail and his bottom lip trembled slightly, the prisoner quickly regained his composure and looked the clerk squarely in the eye as the indictment was read.

"To this bill of indictment, how say you, Guilty, or Not Guilty?" asked the clerk.

"Not guilty," Holmes replied.

"Pleading not guilty, how will you be tried?"

"By God and my country," said Holmes.

"And may God send you a safe deliverance," the clerk concluded.

Edgy and anxious, Shoemaker began the proceedings by immediately requesting a continuance

The back of Holmes' head. Federal Criminologist Arthur MacDonald sites the killer's uneven ears as a sign of his criminal tendencies. (*Philadelphia Public Ledger*; Sept. 24, 1895; Courtesy the Free Library of Philadelphia).

so that he and Rotan might better prepare Holmes' defense. "The time allowed for the preparation of the defence [sic] in this case, commencing with the indictment, has been hopelessly short and inadequate," he said, "for this is a case in which there devolves upon us the absolute necessity of

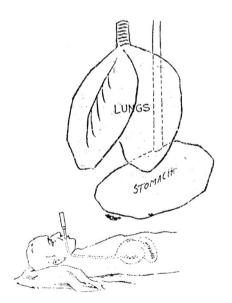

Holmes drew this sketch in an effort to explain how Ben Pitezel could have committed suicide using choloroform.

(*The Philadelphia Inquirer*; October 1895; Courtesy of the Free Library of Philadelphia)

preparing the defence [sic] of three homicide cases." However, District Attorney Graham did not agree, and the judge ordered the trial to continue.

At that point, Shoemaker and Rotan took a totally unexpected and completely unorthodox stand. Rather than continue the case improperly prepared, they asked to withdraw. Shocked, Judge Arnold denied their request and threatened disbarment should they choose not to continue with Holmes' defense.

Jury selection started immediately. The first candidate examined was Enoch Turner, a conductor. After the district attorney turned the questioning over to Holmes and his counsel, they again addressed the

Judge Arnold
(*The Holmes-Pitezel Case*; **Frank Geyer;**
Philadelphia: Publisher's Union, 1896)

Court, saying,

HOLMES: "May it please the Court, I have no intention to ask Mr. Rotan and Mr. Shoemaker to continue in this case when I can see that it is against their own interests, and, bearing that fact in mind, I ask to discharge them from the case. These gentlemen have stood by me during the last year, and I cannot ask them at this time to stay in the trial of the case, where it is against their interest – "

ROTAN: "We do not want the Court to receive the impression that we are deserting this man. He now states that he would rather go on with the case himself."

HOLMES: "If the Court please, I would like a continuance of one day, so that I can get another attorney to attend to my business."

Judge Arnold: "You will have to-morrow [sic] for that purpose. The case will not go on to-day[sic] to its full length...I have ruled the question once, and I mean to abide by my ruling If you desire to examine this juror, do so. Otherwise, we will call another."

At that point, Rotan asked a few question of Mr. Turner, but, after he, Holmes, and Shoemaker conferred, addressed the court again.

ROTAN: "May it please the Court, the defendant in this case says that he intends to examine these witnesses; that he does not want us to interfere with the examination of them, and that that is what he is going to do. Now, as to our position, whether we are here or in any other place, it seems to me, makes very little difference in this case..."

SHOEMAKER: "I cannot conscientiously go on with this case, from the fact that the prisoner has so decided. We must withdraw from the case, however serious the consequences may be. We are seriously embarrassed in this matter, by preparations that we have not been able to make."

Holmes jumped to his counsels' rescue by summarily discharging them, saying he would secure new counsel before the next day's proceedings started and handle jury selection on his own. Judge Arnold refused this action, as well, and cautioned the two attorneys to stay put. However, Shoemaker immediately picked up his hat and left. After a brief explanation as to his untenable position, Rotan followed.

In questioning prospective candidates, Holmes seemed most interested in whether they had been influenced by the sensational exhibits about his supposed crimes being shown at the Dime Museum of Philadelphia. At one point, Holmes asked that the jury selection be continued until the next morning so he might ponder the acceptability of the jurors seated thus far, but that request was denied. Holmes exercised his right of peremptory dismissal of a prospective juror eighteen times. In the end, the jury consisted of:

Robert Kinkaid – Florist

J. G. D. Avril – Printer

Samuel Wood – Yarn Manufacturer

Louise Reese – Farmer

Andrew Hertel – Builder

Robert Chambers – Painter

William P. Hansell – Wagon Builder

James Kenny – Wholesale Clothing Store Owner

Linford Biles – Payroll Clerk for Atlantic Refining

John J. Smith – Train Engineer

Thomas Sloan – Stable Boss

Charles V. Clash – Soap Maker

None of the jury members held a college degree. Except for the payroll clerk, Biles, they were all blue-collar workers who earned their living with their hands. Whether this happened purposely is not known.

The Court adjourned for lunch, after which District Attorney Graham made his opening remarks. Holmes kept his head down, scribbling away on his notepad, and looked up only twice – once when Graham stated chloroform had been injected into Pitezel's stomach after death, and again when the D.A. suggested that Alice Pitezel had been "ruined," that is, raped, by the defendant before her death. After Graham finished, the court was adjourned until 10:00 a.m. Tuesday, October 29th.

The first witness called on Tuesday morning was Jeanette "Dessie" Pitezel, followed by police clerk and photographer, John Townsend. Next on the stand was Eugene Smith who testified regarding the goings-on in the Callowhill Street house. Holmes cross-examined each witness, acting as his own attorney. At one point Holmes requested that all prospective witnesses be removed from the courtroom during each other's testimony and the exception was granted.

Holmes in the dock of the courtroom as he questioned jurors after dismissing his attorneys. (*Philadelphia Inquirer;* Oct. 29, 1895; Courtesy the Free Library of Philadelphia).

153

Dr. William Scott, who responded when Pitezel's body was discovered, indicated that the way the room was arranged, with a slightly raised window and the fireplace flue open, might have been purposely staged to encourage odors from decomposition to go up the chimney.

> "It appeared that the room had been so fixed by allowing the
> draft to blow from these openings made there to the fireplace,
> so that the stench was mostly carried up the chimney...."

Scott also testified that the smashed bottle could not have resulted from an explosion, as the staged scene suggested, since all the residue had fallen *into* the bottle, not away from it. Further questioning dispelled any doubt that Pitezel had intentionally ingested the chloroform found in his stomach.

Holmes pleads his case.
(***Philadelphia Public Ledger;***
Oct. 29, 1895; Courtesy the
Free Library of Philadelphia).

GRAHAM: "Had the chloroform in the stomach been introduced there, could you tell, before death or after death?"

DR. SCOTT: "Finding no inflammation, or no congestion of his stomach, which would have been the results if chloroform had been taken in life, I would say it was put there after death."

This testimony destroyed Holmes' suicide theory, and try though he did, he could not get any of the medical personnel who testified that day to go along with his theory. Before court adjourned for the day, Holmes made a final plea:

"I feel that this case will reach an end quicker by having two sessions a day instead of three, on account of my throat condition. It is utterly impossible for me to attend three sessions without breaking down and becoming sick, for I am subject to sick headache [sic], and I have been suffering with it all day. I think two sessions a day, at least for the next few days, will be sufficient."

The judge denied Holmes' request on the grounds that he had a sequestered jury to consider, as well as witnesses, some of whom had traveled a good distance to be present. Arnold stated he wished no further inconvenience to these people than was absolutely necessary. Court was adjourned until 7:00 p.m.

When everyone returned, there was yet another surprise from the defendant:

HOLMES: "Partly on account of my physical condition, partly because I feel I have been annoyed on the trial unnecessarily by reason of not being expeditious in examining witnesses, and partly because of my counsel being criticized [sic], as alleged, for deserting me, I have sent for them in the last half hour, asking them to come here, and if your Honor sees fit to allow them to come here and consult with me, and if they are willing to go on, I would like to know if the Court is willing that they shall come in the case."

D.A. GRAHAM: "You know whether they are willing to come in or not. You have been in consultation with them. Do you want them here?"

HOLMES: "I have sent for them."

JUDGE ARNOLD: "There are other interests at stake in this case beside your own, in a matter of delay. Twelve jurymen are locked up, and other parties are held as witnesses to their disadvantage, and it has always been the practice here, where a case is of any magnitude, to sit day and night. There is no reason whatever to change that rule. Here come your counsel now. We must economize our time. It is as much a pain and penalty for me as for you to sit here at this time of night."

ROTAN: "May it please your Honor, yesterday, when we were dismissed by our client from this case, we at that time had no expectation of returning to it. We were dismissed entirely. Since that time, however, the defendant in this case has sent for us, and he has talked in reference to the case, the fact that it has been necessary for him to interrupt a great many times, not understanding the tech-

Carrie Pitezel testifies.

(*Philadelphia Public Ledger;*
**Oct. 31, 1895; Courtesy the
Free Library of Philadelphia**).

nicalities of the law, and he felt, probably, he would expedite the case by having his counsel come back. In addition to this, he feels that morning, afternoon and evening sessions would be so wearing upon himself that he could not go on with the trial, indicted as he is, and attend to the progress of the trial. So he asked us to re-appear [sic] in the case."

<u>JUDGE ARNOLD</u>: "I do not think any apology is needed."

<u>ROTAN</u>: "I just wanted to state how it is, your Honor."

So once again, Holmes was represented by Rotan and Shoemaker, and would be for the remainder of the trial. One after the other, witnesses were called and cross-examined: the coroner, attending physicians, neighbors, Fidelity Mutual employees and officers, Dessie and Carrie Pitezel.

Carrie Pitezel was a pitiful sight, drawn and pale, desolate from the loss of her husband and three children. When shown letters that were in Holmes' possession, written by her children but never mailed, she sobbed bitterly. Her testimony was devastating to the defendant's case, but Messrs. Rotan and Shoemaker wisely chose not to cross-examine the weary, bereft woman.

While in Moyamensing Prison, Holmes wrote a letter to Myrta, and that letter was read into the record:

"Dear Mamma[sic]: It is Thanksgiving Day. It finds me in my cell with the feelings strong upon me that I have nothing to be thankful for, not even my life. I took my chances and failed, and my principal regrets are the suffering and disgrace upon you

and all others. I do not think I have to ask you to disbelieve the murder charges. Property interest may necessitate your coming to Philadelphia for the day, but not at present. I expect a two years' sentence, but if I were free to-day [sic] I should never live again as in the past, either with you or anyone else, as I will never run the chances of degrading any woman further. Plummer can explain about the law points of our marriage. In a little time I will write you about the property; only one-half page letters are allowed. Direct care of the superintendent of the prison if you wish to write.   H."

The next witness called was Georgiana Yoke – and that was the name she gave when sworn in. For the first time since the trial began, Holmes broke down. He dropped his head into his hands and sobbed, but quickly composed himself and continued taking his notes. Occasionally during Georgiana's testimony, a sob would escape his firmly sealed lips, but for the most part he remained in control. Many spectators wondered if the whole performance wasn't an act to buy the prisoner some sympathy; either way, there would be none sympathetic to Holmes in that courtroom.

When the district attorney finished questioning Georgiana, attorney Rotan announced that his client insisted on cross-examining this witness. While Holmes questioned her, Georgiana never looked up, never met his gaze. She worried a handkerchief in her lap and murmured her replies just loudly enough to be heard.

Recalled to the stand later, Georgiana stated that while in Burlington she had been visited by one of Holmes' sisters. That sister (whom she does not name) apprised her of the story Holmes had been spreading around Gilmanton of being injured and suffering amnesia.

GRAHAM: "You say you know nothing as to the Wilmette marriage. Do you know anything of another marriage prior to this?"

GEORGIANA: "I had heard he was married."

GRAHAM: "To whom?"

GEORGIANA: "I do not know what her name was, in Gilmington [sic], N. H."

GRAHAM: "Have you talked with him about that wife since your marriage?"

GEORGIANA: "I have."

GRAHAM: "When?"

GEORGIANA: "First in Boston, I believe."

GRAHAM: "What story did he tell his people to excuse him from having married you while his wife at Gilmington [sic], N. H. was still living? What excuse did he give to his own family, or explanation, for having married you under these circumstances?"

ROTAN: "I object."

GRAHAM: "He told them he married this lady while laboring under a state of mental delusion, that he met her in a hospital, that she attended him when sick; she attended him as

159

his nurse; that he became infatuated with her, and married her while in an unconscious condition."

<u>JUDGE ARNOLD</u>: "You may answer the question."

<u>GEORGIANA</u>: "I was not with him when he visited his people."

<u>ROTAN</u>: "Is that admissible, if Mrs. Howard was not there at the time?"

<u>GRAHAM</u>: "Did his sister tell you what had been said?"

<u>GEORGIANA</u>: "She did."

<u>ROTAN</u>: "I object to all of this."

<u>JUDGE ARNOLD</u>: "Objection overruled."

<u>GRAHAM</u>: "Did you talk to him afterwards about what his sister had told you?"

<u>GEORGIANA</u>: "I did."

<u>GRAHAM</u>: "Now we will have the story as you told it to him."

<u>GEORGIANA</u>: "I do not understand what you mean."

<u>GRAHAM</u>: "You have yourself told us that his sister told you what he had said at home, the story by which he excused himself from having married you while his other wife was living, and you talked to him about what his sister had told you. What did you tell him, and what did he say about it? You told him what the sister said. Tell us what that was first, and then what he said."

<u>GEORGIANA</u>: "The sister told me that he had been injured in a wreck, and that he had been taken to a hospital, where he remained for a long time, that I was the patroness of the hospital,

and at last influenced the physicians to perform an operation of saving his mind."

GRAHAM: "He said you had influenced the physician for performing an operation that saved his mind?"

GEORGIANA: "Yes; and that I had married him before he realized who he was, I believe."

GRAHAM: "That you had married him before he realized who he was?"

GEORGIANA: "Yes."

GRAHAM: "Then what?"

GEORGIANA: "And that he had then written to them and had gone to see his father and mother?"

GRAHAM: "Did you meet the woman at Gilmington [sic], N. H.?"

GEORGIANA: "I did not."

GRAHAM: "What did he say to you in explanation of this when you charged him with this false story?"

GEORGIANA: "He had received word that the woman in Gilmington [sic] was dead, and he married me, and he could not then tell me that she was living."

GRAHAM: "In point of fact, she is still living?"

GEORGIANA: "I do not know, but I suppose so."

GRAHAM: "Didn't the sister tell you?"

GEORGIANA: "She did, some months ago."

GRAHAM: "Long since your marriage?"

GEORGIANA: "Yes, sir."

161

GRAHAM: "What explanation did he give to you for having told this strange story to his people about you?"

GEORGIANA: "I do not know that he made any."

GRAHAM: "As a matter of fact, you knew nothing of his having been in a hospital after a wreck, did you?"

GEORGIANA: "I did not."

GRAHAM: "As a matter of fact, you were not the patroness of a hospital in which he was a patient?"

GEORGIANA: "I was not."

GRAHAM: "As a matter of fact, that story was all false, was it not?"

GEORGIANA: "So far as my connection with it is concerned it was."

GRAHAM: "As a matter of fairness to you, at the time you married him, you believed at the time this ceremony was performed you were becoming a lawful wife?"

GEORGIANA: "I did."

GRAHAM: "Or you would not have married him?"

GEORGIANA: "I would not."

ᐧ

If Carrie Pitezel's testimony devastated Holmes' case, Detective Frank Geyer's time on the stand sealed the killer's fate. In a firm voice, the man told of his search along Holmes' confusing path and finding the bodies of the three children.

After testifying, Carrie collapsed in the district attorney's office. She is aided by a nurse as Dessie looks on. (*New York World;* Nov. 2, 1895; courtesy New Hampshire Historical Society).

"Devils may be able to understand how that man cut and burned that innocent child [Howard]," said Graham, "but it is not within the ken of men to understand it."

The tears that sprang to Geyer's eyes occasionally during his testimony destroyed any hope Holmes may have harbored of garnering any sympathy from the jury. Though D. A. Graham attempted to enter evidence and testimony proving that Holmes had killed the children as well as their father, Judge Arnold squelched that motion. "...this prisoner is now on trial for the killing of Benjamin F. Pitezel in the city of Philadelphia, and that is the case, and the only case, to be tried here." This ruling effectively silenced over thirty witnesses that Geyer had lined up to testify in that regard. It also barred admittance of the artifacts collected by Detective Geyer on his grueling search...a tiny jawbone,

The stove in which Holmes burned Howard's body was packed and shipped to Philadelphia, but Judge Arnold would not allow it into evidence.

(*New York World;* Nov. 4, 1895; Courtesy New Hampshire Historical Society).

the small teeth, the scorched clothing of the children. After calling a few witnesses to tie up loose ends, the district attorney rested the state's case against H. H. Holmes.

At this point, an outwardly confident Rotan rose and presented what many of the newspapers called "a bold bluff:"

"May it please this Honorable Court, Mr. Shoemaker and myself have just had a consultation with the defendant in reference to the defence [sic]. We feel that from our inability, as stated to you on Monday, to bring a number of very important witnesses from other parts, that it is advisable for us to close the case now and put in no testimony whatever. We do this, may it please your Honor, also from the fact that we feel that the Commonwealth has utterly failed to make out their case. However, this proposition comes from us with the proviso, if your Honor does not hasten us on with the speeches. We have not had time to prepare our speeches, and if your Honor is willing that the speeches for the defence [sic] shall not be heard until to-morrow [sic] at any time, we will try to save as much public time in reference to the case as possible."

Judge Arnold and D.A. Graham agreed and court was adjourned until 10 a.m. Saturday morning.

A visibly weary jury filed into the box and took their seats. Mr. Rotan again took the floor to announce that Shoemaker was under a doctor's care caused by "a complete state of nervous prostration," and would be unable to attend the proceedings. He asked the Court to go on with the case, as that was Mr. Shoemaker's wish. Judge Arnold agreed.

Then Rotan began a plea to present his closing argument last. Usually, since the state has the burden of proof, the district attorney is allowed to be the last voice the jurors hear before deliberation. However, Graham waived that right and agreed to allow Rotan to speak last.

The district attorney's closing argument covers fifty pages in the published transcript of the trial. He went back over every point and nuance that could help paint Holmes as the killer he was. After Graham had finished, Judge Arnold dismissed everyone for lunch. With all the players fed and comfortable, and court resumed, it was Rotan's turn to state the case for Herman W. Mudgett, alias Dr. H. H. Holmes.

Though knowing his case was hopeless, Rotan made the best he could of the scant defense with which he had to work. To his credit, his closing statement was a full twenty-five pages of the transcript – exactly half as long as the district attorney's. That Rotan kept his argument going for such a long period of time, given what little he could offer as to his client's innocence, is a credit to his dedication. He ended his summation at 4:30 p.m. with the following statement:

"I now let this case go to you with a great deal of confidence – so much confidence that we have not put in a defence [sic]. We feel that the Commonwealth has failed in removing that reasonable doubt to which the prisoner is entitled, and that we can safely rely upon this case going to you and your rendering a verdict of not guilty. This poor man has indeed suffered long, and undoubtedly will suffer, if not here, in other places, for a long time to come, and I only ask of you that you decide this case upon the facts here presented, which, if you do, we have no fear but that you will render a verdict of acquittal."

All that remained now in that sensational trial was for Judge Arnold to instruct the jury and send them to deliberate. His lengthy instructions took up over twenty pages of the transcript. At 5:40 p.m., Holmes fate was delivered into the hands of the jury. Holmes was returned to his cell, a smile on his face despite the fact he was visibly anxious. Judge Arnold said he would remain in the building until midnight, at which time he would go home if there was not yet a verdict, and return the next morning at 10:00 a.m. To the surprise of none, the jury did not take that long to agree on a verdict.

The New York World reported interviewing several lawyers who had attended or followed the case, and all of them thought that the jury would bring back a verdict of not guilty, meaning "not proven."

However, a jury expert who had attended the trial predicted a guilty verdict.

As he awaited his fate, even though every minute must have seemed interminable, Holmes managed to maintain his composure. He had been assured by his attorneys and his guards that he would be acquitted. However, one guard made the comment that "it was most painful to watch him."

At 8:40 p.m., Judge Arnold again took his place behind the bench, and Holmes was brought in and placed in the cage. The opposing counsels returned to the chairs they had occupied throughout the trial, reporters rushed to seats in the gallery, and the jury filed into the box to deliver their decision.

Holmes stood erect, staring blankly at the jury, his face deathly pale. He repeatedly moistened his lips with his tongue.

Then the deep-voiced court clerk said: Jurors, look upon the prisoner; prisoner, look upon the jurors. How say you, gentlemen of the jury, do you find the prisoner at the bar, Herman W. Mudgett, alias H. H. Holmes, guilty of the murder of Benjamin F. Pitezel or not guilty?"

The foreman stood and said in a clear voice, "Guilty of murder in the first degree."

As these words echoed through the stark courtroom, Holmes took out his watch, opened it, and then shut it with a loud snap. He cleared his throat and gripped the bar of the cage a bit tighter, then slowly sat down.

One *New York World* reporter stated, "The red spots faded away from his cheeks and his eyes opened wider and wider. With his fixed stare and his half-open mouth, he looked like a listening maniac. He was not thinking. His face was a moving picture of hopelessness and despair."

At Rotan's request, the jury was polled. Holmes scribbled each name in the margin of a newspaper as they were called. One of the jurors later revealed that their verdict had been reached before the door closed behind them for deliberation. It was only for the sake of decency that they waited until after dinner to announce their decision.

The verdict was formally recorded and Judge Arnold thanked the jury for their service. Rotan made a motion for a new trial, which would eventually be denied. With that, the court adjourned and the trial of the century was ended.

∾

As the gloom gathered inside Moyamensing Prison that night, the newly-convicted murderer prepared to move from the cell that had been his home for over a year. He could no longer remain in the "untried department" of the prison, but must now be relocated to a cell block reserved for convicted killers. Holmes sat at a small table strewn with notes he had written during the trial, his plain dinner of tea and bread untouched. On the floor beside him lay his bed, a bundle of straw inside a bag of ticking. Three gray army blankets and a straw pillow completed his sleeping accommodations. In one corner was Holmes' library – a stack of books that included *Witter's English*

This diagram of Moyamensing Prison shows the small area that was Holmes' world during his incarceration. On the second row, the third cell on the left was where Holmes was held from the time of his arrest until the end of his trial. On the bottom tier, the third door on the right was his home following his conviction and until he was executed. The rectangle in the center of the corridor is where the gallows was constructed for his execution.

(*Philadelphia Inquirer*; Nov. 4, 1895; Courtesy of the Free Library of Philadelphia)

and German Primer, The Earl's Error (Charlotte M. Braeme), *Under the Red Flag* (M. E. Braddon), *At a Girl's Mercy* (Jean Kate Ludlun), and the October editions of *McClure* and *Munsey* magazines.

On the wall over the table, Holmes had written: *Ah, mon Dieu! Que la vie est amerque*! The translation is "Ah, my God! How bitter life is!" A short distance away, he had also written "Laugh and the world will laugh with you; sigh, and you sigh alone."

With the guilty verdict in, the move to the first tier, where Holmes would be held until his execution date, was made immediately. The killer had the scant solace of knowing that his diet would improve significantly while in that "death-watch" cell. No longer restricted to the plain food of common minor criminals, Holmes would be able to select his own menus until his execution.

Holmes stayed up late after being relocated to the first tier. His jailers pleaded with him to eat his dinner, but Holmes replied that nothing was so unwise as to eat when agitated. When he had recovered a bit from the shock of hearing his sentence, he ate a simple meal, wrapped himself in a heavy gray army blanket, lay down on his bed of straw, and dozed off.

For a solid week he had been working on his case until the wee hours, getting only a couple hours sleep each night. And so Holmes slept through the morning jailers' watch and into the afternoon, finally waking at around three o'clock. He ate his breakfast, chatted for a short while with the guards, and then turned his attention to preparing arguments for a new trial.

The guards who were interviewed reported Holmes had regained his "splendid nerve" very quickly and were inclined to believe the rapid change in demeanor indicated his guilt. "They notice that the guiltiest prisoners are usually the bravest," reported the *New York World* on November 4th, "if murderers can be called brave."

As Holmes prepared for an imminent visit from his mother, the papers commented on Holmes' effect on women and on the number of females present throughout the trial. Some were young and pretty; others were matrons. But young and old alike spent most of their time gazing upon the prisoner, seeming mesmerized by the man. "None of them drifted in from mere curiosity, or without effort," reported the *New York World*, "for the general public has throughout been excluded from the trial, and those who got in were compelled to know and ask admission of important public officials." In the meantime, Georgiana had returned to Denver, planning to have her "marriage" to Holmes dissolved.

By April 9th, 1896, Holmes had already written three different confessions, none of them admitting to any crime more serious than fraud. But less than a month before his execution, Holmes sold the exclusive rights to his final confession to William Randolph Hearst for $10,000. In this confession, he would take responsibility for twenty-seven murders, but the total of Holmes' heinous crimes died with him on the gallows. The murders he committed must number far more than the admitted twenty-seven. Most people who have studied his case put the number of deaths attributable to the man at somewhere between two to three hundred.

The Philadelphia Inquirer printed a half-page announcement of the upcoming scoop on Friday, April 10th 1896, stating the confession would be printed in full in their Sunday edition. In huge text was the following:

Holmes Confesses Many Murders

The Most Fearful and Horrible Murderer Ever

Known in the Annals of Crime

First and Only Complete Confession

The Most Remarkable Story of Murder and

Inhuman Villainy Ever Made Public

Conviction Lies in Every Line

And to be sure, Holmes did not disappoint the ravenous followers of his case. The preamble to his confession was particularly chilling, his crimes mechanically laid out as though they were a list of chores finally completed.

"I am convinced that since my imprisonment I have changed woefully and gruesomely from what I formerly was in feature and figure...My features are assuming nothing more or less than a pronounced Satanical cast."

H. H. Holmes

Chapter Fourteen

The Final Confession

Holmes looked up from his writing and stared at the cold white walls of his prison cell. He shivered from the chill, the stone walls greedily devouring any hint of warmth that might have wafted through. His gaze dropped to the paper lying before him and he read the words he had just penned,

"Yes, I was born with the devil in me. I could not help the fact that I was a murderer no more than the poet can help the inspiration to song, nor the ambition of an intellectual man to be great. I was born with the evil one standing as my sponsor beside the bed where I was ushered into the world, and he has been with me since. The inclination

Though it was never proven, and Holmes certainly did not confess it, he was suspected of killing Blanche LaMont, a neighbor of his wife, Myrta's, in Wilmette.

(*The Chicago Times;* **September 1895; Courtesy of the Abraham Lincoln Presidential Library)**

to murder came to me as naturally as the inspiration to do good comes to other men."

He again picked up his pen, dipped the point in the bottle of ebony ink, and continued writing with urgency.

"It was when I returned home to visit my family after securing my medical degree, and our boy [Robert, his and Clara's son] was then but a youngster playing about with other lads of his own size and age, that I was seized with a wild desire to destroy.

"So, I called him in from the road where he was frolicking about like an innocent with a lot of other lads, and took him out to a rear barn.

"I don't know what it was that possessed me, but I took a surgical knife along with me. It was not the sudden impulse nor the maddening desire of a father, seeing his child about to grow up and enter a world of sorrow and sin, that led me to the deed. No, it was not that. It was simply the craving of the murderer within me that inspired me to make a subject of my little one.

"I noticed that there was a terrible look of fear on the little fellow's face as I took him into the barn, and he trembled as I took the knife and told him to undress.

"I had often thought since that it was like the look of the scared rabbit laid on the operating table, as its pitiful eyes search the group about him, and see them all intent only on the anticipated incision.

Holmes in his cell at Moyamensing Prison.

(*Philadelphia Inquirer;* **March 17, 1896; courtesy the Free Library of Philadelphia).**

"During the past few months the desire has been repeatedly expressed that I make a detailed confession of all the graver crimes that have with such marvelous skill been traced out and brought home to me. I have been tried for murder, convicted, sentenced, and the first step of my execution upon May seventh, namely, the reading of my death warrant, has been carried out, and it now seems a fitting time, if ever to make known the details of the twenty-seven murders, of which it would be useless to longer say I am not guilty, in the face of the overwhelming amount of proof that has been brought together, not only in one but in each and every case; and because in this confession I speak only of cases that have been thus investigated and of no others, I trust it will not give rise to supposition that I am still guilty of other murders which I am withholding...

A word as to the motives or causes that have led to the commission of these many crimes and I will proceed to the most difficult and distasteful task of my life, the setting forth in all its horrid nakedness the recital of the premeditated killing of twenty-seven human beings and the unsuccessful attempts to take the lives of six others, thus branding myself as the most detestable criminal of modern time – a task so hard and distasteful that beside it the certainty that in a few days I am to be hanged by the neck until I am dead seems but a pastime.

After Warner had installed his glass-bending furnace, Holmes stepped outside the oven, slammed the door, and gassed the inventor.

(*Philadelphia Inquirer*, July 1895; Courtesy of the Free Library of Philadelphia)

"I am convinced that since my imprisonment I have changed woefully and gruesomely from what I was formerly in feature and figure. My features are assuming a pronounced Satanical cast. I have become afflicted with that dread disease, rare but terrible, with which physicians are acquainted, but over which they have no control whatsoever. That disease is a malformation or distortion of the osseous parts...My head and face are gradually assuming an elongated shape. I believe fully that I am growing to resemble the devil – that the similitude is almost completed.

"Acquired homicidal mania, all other causes, save the occasional opportunity for pecuniary gain having by others been excluded for me, is the only constant cause, and in advancing it at this time I do not do so with the expectation of a mitigation of public condemnation, or that it will in any way react in my favor. Had this been my intention I should have considered it at the time of my trial, and had it used as my defense.

"All criminologists who have examined me here seem to be unanimous in the opinions that they have formed, although one inexplicable condition presents itself, viz.: that while committing the crimes these symptoms were not present, but commenced to develop after my arrest.

"Ten years ago I was thoroughly examined by four men of marked ability and by them pronounced as being both mentally and physically a normal and healthy man [the reason for that examination is not revealed]. To-day [sic] I have every attribute of a degenerate – a moral idiot. Is it possible that the crimes, instead of being the result of these abnormal conditions, are in themselves the occasion of the degeneracy?

"Even at the time of my arrest in 1894 no defects were noticeable under the searching Bertillon system of measurements to which I was subjected, but later, and more noticeably within the past few months these defects have increased with startling rapidity, as is made known to me by each succeeding examination until I have become thankful that I have no longer a glass with which to note my rapidly deteriorat-

Sketch of Ben Pitezel.
(*Chicago Times-Herald;* **Sept. 14, 1895; Courtesy the Abraham Lincoln Presidential Library**).

ing condition, though nature, ever kind, provides in this, as in the ordinary forms of insanity where the sufferer believes himself always sane, so that, unless called to my attention, I do not notice my infirmity nor suffer therefrom. The principal defects that have thus far developed and which are all established signs of degeneracy, are a decided prominence upon one side of my head and a corresponding diminution upon the other side, a marked deficiency of one side of my nose and of one ear, together with an abnormal increase of each upon the opposite side, a difference of one and one-half inches in the length of my arms and an equal shortening of one leg from knee to heel; also a most malevolent distortion of one side of my face and of my face and of one yes – so marked and terrible that in writing of it for publication, Hall Caine, although I wore a beard at the time to conceal it as best I could, described that side of my face as marked by a deep line of crime and being that of a devil – so apparent that an expert criminologist in the employ of the United States Government who had never previously seen me said within thirty seconds after entering my cell: 'I know you are guilty.'

A sketch depicting one of Holmes' many murders.
(*The Philadelphia Inquirer;* **April 12, 1896; Courtesy
of the Free Library of Philadelphia)**

"Would it not, then, be the height of folly for me to die without speaking if only for the purpose of justifying these scientific deductions and accrediting what is due to those whom society owes so much for bringing me to justice?

"The first taking of human life that is attributed to me is the case of Dr. Robert Leacock of New Baltimore, Mich., a friend and former schoolmate. I knew that his life was insured for a large sum and after enticing him to Chicago I killed him by giving him an overwhelming dose of laudanum...The risk and excitement attendant upon the collection of the forty-thousand dollars of insurance were very insignificant matters compared with the torturing thought that I had taken human life.

"This will be understood that before my constant wrong-doing, I had become wholly deaf to the promptings of conscience...Later, like the man-eating tiger of the tropical jungle, whose appetite for blood has once been aroused, I roamed around the world seeking whom I could destroy.

"My second victim was Dr. Russell, a tenant in the Chicago building recently renamed 'The Castle.' During a controversy concerning the non-payment of rent due me, I struck him to the floor with a heavy chair, when he with one cry for help, ending in a groan of anguish, ceased to breathe. [Holmes sold Russell's body to the Chicago medical school].

"The third death was to a certain extent due to a criminal operation. A man and woman are cognizant of and partially responsible for both the operation and death. The victim was Mrs. Julia L. Connor. A reference to almost any newspaper of August, 1895, will give the minute details of the horrors of this case, as they were worked out by the detectives before, making it necessary to repeat it here, save to add that the death of the child Pearl, her little daughter, who is the fourth victim, was caused by poison.

"The fifth murder, that of Rodgers, of West Morgantown, Va., occurred in 1888, at which time I was boarding there for a few weeks. Learning that the man had some money I induced him to go upon a fishing trip with me, and being successful in allaying his suspicions, I finally ended his life by a sudden blow upon the head with an oar.

"The sixth case is that of Charles Cole, a Southern speculator. After considerable correspondence this man came to Chicago, and I enticed him into the castle, where, while I was engaging him in conversation, a confederate struck him a most vicious blow upon the head with a piece of gas pipe. So heavy was the blow it not only caused his death without a groan and hardly a movement, but it crushed his skull to such an extent that his body was almost useless to the party who bought the body.

"A domestic, named Lizzie, was the seventh victim. She, for a time, worked in the Castle restaurant and I soon learned that Quinlan was paying her too close attention and fearing lest it should progress so far that it would necessitate his leaving my employ, I thought it wise to end the life of the girl. This I did by calling her to my office and suffocating her in the vault...she being the first victim to die therein.

"The eighth, ninth and tenth cases are Mrs. Sarah Cook, her unborn child, and Miss Mary Haracamp, of Hamilton, Canada. In 1888 Mr. Frank Cook became a tenant in the Castle. He was engaged to be married [to Sarah]...[After marrying], they kept house in the Castle, and for a time I boarded with them. Shortly Miss Mary Haracamp..., a niece of Mrs. Cook..., entered my employ as a stenographer. But Mrs. Cook and her niece had access to all the rooms by means of a master key and one evening while I was busily engaged preparing my last victim for shipment, the door suddenly opened and they stood before me...Before they had recovered from the horror of the sight, they were within the fatal vault...

"Soon after this Miss Emmeline Cigrand...was sent to me by a Chicago typewriter firm [this is not true; Holmes pursued her from the Gold Cure alcoholism institute]... A man visited her from time to time while she was in my employ. She was finally engaged to him [another lie; the man Emmeline became 'engaged' to was Holmes, under an alias]... I endeavored upon several occasions to take the life of the young man and failing in this I finally resolved that I would kill her instead, and upon the day of their wedding, even after cards had been sent out...she came to my office to bid me goodbye. While there I asked her to step inside the vault for some papers for me...only to learn that the vault would never again [be] opened until she had ceased to suffer the tortures of a slow and lingering death.

"My next [victim] was a very beautiful young woman named Rosine Van Jassand, whom I induced to come into my fruit and confection store, and, once within my power, I compelled her to live with me there for a time, threatening her with death if she appeared before any of my customers. A little later I killed her by administering ferro-cyanide of potassium.

"Robert Latimer, a man who had for some years been in my employ as janitor, was my next victim. He [knew] of certain insurance work I had engaged in and when he sought to extort money from me, his own death and the sale of his body was the recompense meted out to him. I confined him in the secret room and slowly starved him to death. The partial excavation in the walls of this room found by the police was caused by Latimer's endeavoring to escape by tearing away the solid brick and mortar with his unaided fingers.

"The fourteenth case is that of Miss Anna Betts, and was caused by my purposely substituting a poisonous drug in a prescription that had been sent to my drug store to be compounded.

"The death of Miss Gertrude Conner, though not the next in order of occurrence, is so similar to the last that a description of one suffices for both, save in this case Miss Conner left Chicago immediately but did not die until she had reached her home in Muscatine.

"The sixteenth murder is that of Miss Kate [last name unknown], of Omaha, a young woman owning much valuable real estate in Chicago, where I acted as her agent. I caused Miss Kate...to convert her holdings into cash...I asked her to look about my offices and finally to look within the vault, and, having once passed that fatal door, she never came forth alive. She did not die at once, however, and her anger when first she realized she was deprived of her liberty, then her offer of the entire forty thousand dollars in exchange for same and finally her prayers are something terrible to remember.

"The next death was that of a man named Warner, the originator of the Warner Glass Bending Company, and here again a very large sum of money was realized, which prior to his death had been deposited in two Chicago banks, nearly all of which I secured by means of two checks, made out and properly signed by him for a small sum each. To these I later added the word thousand...[and] promptly realized the money. [The kiln in the basement] was so arranged that in less than a minute after turning on a jet of crude oil atomized with steam the entire kiln would be filled with a colorless flame, so intensely hot iron would be melted therein. It was into this kiln that I induced Mr. Warner to go with me, under pretense of wishing certain minute explanations of the process, and then stepping outside, as he believed to get some tools, I closed the door and turned on the oil and steam to their full extent. In a short time not even the bones of my victim remained.

"[The next victim] was a wealthy banker named Rodgers...to cause him to go in the Castle and within the secret room under the pretense that our patents were there was easily brought about, more so to force him to sign checks and drafts for seventy thousand dollars, which we had prepared...Finally by alternately starving him and nauseating him with the gas he was made to sign the securities, all of which were converted into money...

"The nineteenth case is that of a woman, whose name has passed from my memory, who came to the Castle restaurant to board. This was done by my administering chloroform while [Quinlan] controlled her violent struggles. It was the body of this woman within the long coffin-shaped box that was taken from the Castle late in 1893.

"The Williams sisters come next." The circumstances of this case are given in detail earlier in this book and need not be reiterated.

"A man who came to Chicago to attend the Chicago Exposition, but whose name I cannot recall, was my next victim...I decided to bury the body in the basement of the house that I formerly owned near the corner of Seventy-Fourth and Honore streets in Chicago.

"After Miss Williams' death I found among her papers an insurance policy made in her favor by her brother Baldwin Williams of Leadville, Col. I therefore went to that city early in 1894, and, having found him, took his life by shooting him, it being believed I had done so in self-defense. A little later, when the assignment of the policy to which I had forged Miss

Holmes kills Pitezel girls.

1 – The children now realized their predicament
and began to beg piteously for mercy.

2 – Holmes arranged a rubber hose to the gas jet and put the end of
the same through the hole into the trunk and turned on the hose.

(*Philadelphia Inquirer;* Oct. 30, 1895; Courtesy
Free Library of Philadelphia)

Williams' name was presented to John M. Maxwell, of Leadville, the administrator of the Williams estate, it was honored and the money paid.

"Benjamin F. Pitezel [and his children] come next. It will be understood that from the first hour of our acquaintance, even before I knew he had a family who would later afford me additional victims for the gratification of my bloodthirstiness, I intended to kill him, and all my subsequent care of him and his, as well as my apparent trust in him by placing in his name large amounts of property, were steps taken to gain his confidence and that of this family so when the time was ripe they would the more readily fall into my hands.

"[After killing Alice and Nettie in Toronto, I went to Ogdensburg, from there to Burlington, Vermont, when I hired a furnished house for

**Holmes kills Howard. He held the boy between his knees, wrapped
his fingers about his throat, and slowly strangled the boy.
(*Philadelphia Inquirer;* Oct. 30, 1895; Courtesy
Free Library of Philadelphia)**

Mrs. Pitezel's use, and a few days prior to my arrest in Boston I wrote her a letter in which I directed her to carry a bottle of dynamite that I had previously left in the basement so arranged that in taking it to the third story of the house it would fall from her hands, and not only destroy her life, but that of her two remaining children, who I knew would be with her at the time. This was my last act, and happily, did not have a fatal termination.

"It would now seem a very fitting time for me to express regret or remorse...To do so with the expectation of even one person who has read this confession to the end, believing that in my depraved nature there is room for such feelings, is I fear, to expect more than would be granted. I can at least, and do refrain, from calling forth such a criticism by openly inviting it."

"I am Jack!"

H. H. Holmes,
(as rope snaps his neck)

Chapter Fifteen

Death Watch

Over the six-month period following his conviction and leading up to his execution, Holmes was alternately resigned to his fate and manic with plans intended to rescue him from the gallows. Confession truly being good for the soul, Holmes' greetings became cheerier, his eyes brighter, his step livelier once he had unburdened his conscience.

Holmes now set about putting his affairs in order as best he could. He deflected numerous requests from surgeons and scientists for permission to assist at his autopsy and retain possession of various parts of his anatomy. Even though he doubted that any of his family would care to see him given a decent burial, he still wanted his body intact and given a Christian send-off. Eventually, Holmes was assured that the "ostentatious searchers after knowledge" would not be given the opportunity to satisfy their "morbid curiosity" by experimenting with his body. Sheriff

Father Dailey.
(*The Philadelphia Inquirer;*
**April 14, 1896; Courtesy the
Free Library of Philadelphia).**

Clement informed him of a law which Holmes or any member of his family could invoke to prevent holding a post-mortem examination.

As the snow began to melt and the temperature in his cell grew a bit warmer, Holmes prepared himself to meet his maker. On April 16th, he cordially welcomed a group of Catholic priests into his cell. The priests' visit was occasioned by Holmes' desire to be baptized into the Catholic Church. After a brief conversation, Fr. P. J. Dailey, pastor of the Church of the Annunciation, donned the traditional white surplice and stole always worn during a baptism. Accompanying him were a Fr. De Cantillon, Fr. Higgins, and Fr. McCabe.

Speaking slowly and solemnly, his eyes locked on Fr. Dailey's face, Holmes recited the confession of the faith required by the Church, a creed written by the scribes at Nicea in the sixth century A.D. and still used today.

As Fr. Dailey pronounced the words of the baptismal ceremony, chilled drops of holy water spattered across Holmes' skin, and with that, he became a member of the Catholic Church. The priests stayed over an hour, chatting with their new convert.

After they left, Holmes sat on his bunk, gazing at a cross on the wall that he had fashioned from chains. He took great solace in Fr. Dailey's assurance that the Church was for all, saint as well as sinner.

Other Christians were also concerned with Holmes' immortal soul. He saw an article in the *Inquirer* about Rev. Henry S. Clubb, pastor of Christ Church, who had made a plea on Holmes' behalf while delivering a sermon on the Prodigal Son. "But the State of Pennsylvania proposes not to follow the teachings of Christ in the parable," he said, "but to take this repentant brother and hang him by the neck until he is dead." Clubb then continued on to say that with the commutation of Holmes sentence to life imprisonment, the killer could then contribute to the financial support of the remaining Pitezel family.

Holmes leapt on this opportunity and, on April 30, one week before his scheduled execution, he sent appeals to Carrie Pitezel to speak with the governor on his behalf. Neither Carrie nor the governor was interested.

Appalled, Holmes fielded requests from people who wanted to observe his autopsy, as well as some to acquire various of his organs after execution. One museum offered Holmes a substantial sum for his heart and skull to put on exhibit, and a New York physician was equally generous in putting a price on his brain. Holmes denied them all.

The prison was inundated with requests for permission to observe the execution. Holmes was relieved to learn that Sheriff Clement, as well as the prison officials, decided only to allow such witnesses as were provided by law.

"I am innocent. I had no insurance on any of those settlers," says Holmes in this political cartoon following the massacre at Jackson Hole.

(*Philadelphia Inquirer;* April 2, 1896; Courtesy the Free Library of Philadelphia).

Holmes became obsessed with proving that he was not responsible for Howard Pitezel's death. He dedicated most of the money he received from his confession and other available funds to Rotan's efforts to lo-

"Shake, Pard!"
This cartoon appeared following the massacre at Jackson's Hole.
(*Philadelphia Inquirer;* **April 15, 1896; courtesy**
the Free Library of Philadelphia).

cate witnesses who could prove his innocence of that crime. Holmes knew he would still be hanged for the murder of the boy's father, but was frantic to redeem himself of Howard's murder. He became moody and preoccupied, and was placed on suicide watch, meaning that there was at least one guard posted outside his cell to watch his every movement.

The day after his confession, Holmes read in the *Inquirer* about a letter that had arrived at the prison addressed to him. Inside was a druggist's powder paper filled with what was believed to be arsenic. The letter stated, "H. H. Holmes: In mercy to you I send this. Take it and die, and may God have mercy on your soul." The offering never reached his hands.

Just four days before his execution, *The Philadelphia Inquirer* reported on two different horoscopes that Holmes had in his possession. The prisoner, it said, "...has a horoscope which he says shows that he will die a natural death. But he also has a 'horror-scope' which indicates that he will die by being 'delicately strangled between the head and shoulders.'"

By his final Sunday in this world, Holmes was resigned to the reality that his life would soon end. Fr. Dailey brightened his day by bringing communion. After the priest left, Holmes addressed his breakfast with little appetite, his imminent death dampening any enthusiasm for mortal pleasures. He finished the rest of that day reading and writing. At that point, wanting at least one familiar face nearby when he was sent into eternity, Holmes requested that Fr. Dailey be present at his hanging.

Holmes showed great contempt for the jailers and others around him in the prison, greeting their opinions with derisive little laughs. He was certain no prisoner at Moyamensing Prison had ever been so thoroughly disliked, but eventually the utter friendlessness of his position began to weigh on him. At the sound of approaching footsteps, his heart would jump in anticipation. Most often, however, the footsteps faded into the distance, leaving him dejected. All he had now to look forward to were the daily visits of his lawyer, Mr. Rotan, and frequent visits from Fr. Dailey.

On Monday, Holmes could not elude the sounds of the hammers and saws that were assembling the gallows that would be used for his execution. Only about sixty feet removed from his cell, each blow of metal on wood was a reminder of how soon his world would go silent.

Holmes knew all that was being said of him; how he had captured the title of the most fiendish killer in the annals of American history. Every day, it seemed the press coined yet another catch phrase to describe him, from "that prince of insurance swindlers," to the "king of fabricators," and finally "the versatile butcher."

The Chicago Times Herald said "...to parallel such a career one must go back to past ages and to the time of the Borgias or Brinvilliers, and even these were not such human monsters as Holmes seems to have been. He is a prodigy of wickedness, a human demon, a being so unthinkable to the mind that no novelist could dare to invent such a character."

The Chicago Inter Ocean stated that "a sigh of relief will go up from the whole country with the knowledge that Herman Mudgett, or Henry H. Holmes, man or monster, has been exterminated – much the same as a plague to humanity would be wiped out."

After the priests left him on the eve of his execution, Holmes looked at the night watchman, George Weaver, saying "I don't know where I'll sleep tomorrow night. But nobody knows that."

He slipped between the rough blankets on his cot, the straw penetrating the coarse ticking, scratching his skin. He gazed at the little table in his room, his eyes passing over the neatly folded papers to linger on the photograph of his beloved Georgiana. The last clothes he would

Holmes cell at Moyamensing Prison.
(*Philadelphia Inquirer;* **March 17, 1896; courtesy**
the Free Library of Philadelphia).

ever don, those that would become his shroud, lay ready for the morning. He rolled over and, despite his discomfort, fell instantly asleep.

The day watch, John Henry, roused him at 6:00 a.m. Once awake,
Holmes asked cheerily, "Good morning. Is it six o'clock already?"

Henry asked, "How are you this morning?"

"First-rate. I was very tired last night and was glad to get to bed,"
Holmes said, "I never slept better in my life."

Holmes began to dress, going about his daily grooming as though
he hadn't a care in the world. He took particular care with dressing,
wanting to be immaculate for his send-off. He wrote several letters:
one to each of the women he had married, a few to various relatives,

Holmes writes his final letters to family in the shadow of the noose.
(*The Philadelphia Inquirer;*
May 6, 1896; Courtesy the Free Library of Philadelphia).

and messages for friends and family of some of his victims. Finally, he wrote his will.

Frs. Dailey and McPake arrived, and Holmes interrupted his writings to take his final communion with them. After they left, he ate a hearty breakfast.

When Rotan arrived, he scrutinized his client, nodded his head in approval, and said, "You're all right. You look lots better than you did last night."

Holmes responded by holding out his left arm, fingers splayed, saying, "See if I tremble."

He didn't.

The condemned man reviewed his burial plans with Rotan, who reported that a man had come to his office the previous day and offered $5,000 for Holmes' body. Rotan had the man thrown out.

Remembering his own history of body snatching, Holmes was horrified the same fate awaited his corpse, and said, "Thank you. I'll see that no one gets my body, either by buying it or stealing it."

Holmes scribbled a final fond message to his attorney and friend, and handed the note to Rotan.

"I will never touch pen to paper again," he said.

∾

Fifty-one people assembled to witness the execution at Sheriff Clement's invitation. Among those present by 9:00 o'clock were Detective Frank Geyer and Fidelity Mutual president L. G. Fouse. Though angry to learn that his inspectors had sneaked some of their friends into the crowd, the sheriff opted not to eject them. The mass of morbidly curious spectators outside the prison numbered as high as a thousand.

∾

Holmes' final walk. He is braced on either side by one of his priests, with the warden and district attorney bringing up the rear. (*The Philadelphia Inquirer;* May 8, 1896; Courtesy the Free Library of Philadelphia).

From the gallows, Holmes declared his innocence.
(*The New York World;* May 8, 1896; courtesy of
the New Hampshire Historical Society).

At 10:00 o'clock, the cell door was opened and Holmes stepped out into the corridor, flanked by the two priests. Holmes turned to the expanse between the north and south cell blocks and got his first glimpse of the gallows. Supported by his priests and his attorney, he took the first step toward his execution. A short flight of stairs led him down to the pavement, on the same tarmac as the device that would end his life. The scaffold spanned the distance between the two cell blocks, enormous and forbidding.

Superintendent Perkins and Sheriff Clement walked side-by-side up the steps to the gallows. The priests followed, chanting the *Miserere*.

Holding a crucifix in his hand, Holmes took the first step of his climb to death. When he reached the platform, he walked to the edge of the scaffold, gazed at the eager crowd, and rested his hands on the waist-high rail.

"Gentlemen, I have very few words to say. In fact, I would make no remarks at this time were it not for the feeling that if I did not speak it would imply that the extent of the wrongdoing I am guilty of in taking human life is the killing of two women. They died by my hands as the results of criminal operations (most likely abortion). I also wish to state, so that no chance of misunderstanding may exist hereafter, that I am not guilty of taking the lives of any of the Pitezel family, either the three children or the father, Benjamin F. Pitezel, for whose death I am now to be hanged. I have never committed murder.

"That is all I have to say."

He turned as he spoke the last sentence and placed his hand on Rotan's shoulder, smiling as he said,

"Good-bye, Sam. You have done all you could."

He hugged his attorney, whispered a few words in his ear, and knelt before the priests. The three prayed together for a couple of minutes, then Holmes rose steadily to his feet, shook hands with the two pastors, buttoned his coat, and nodded to the prison officials.

As the priests resumed chanting, Holmes' hands were drawn behind his back and handcuffed. He gazed solemnly at the last two faces he would see in this life, Sheriff Clement and Superintendent Perkins, as the black hood was slipped over his head.

"Take your time about it," he said. "You know I am in no hurry."

With the black hood over his head, Holmes awaits death.
(*The New York World;* **May 8, 1896; courtesy of
the New Hampshire Historical Society).**

He felt the noose against his neck, felt it drawn tight. His heart pounding, he spoke his last words, voice muffled by the cloth.

"Good-bye, good-bye, everybody."

The superintendent dropped a handkerchief, the signal for the executioner, and at 10:12 ½, the black boards upon which he stood parted and Holmes' felt the floor give way beneath him.

His final sensation in this life was the jerk of the rope that snapped his neck. His descent stopped abruptly, his head knocked to one side, and the force sent his body swinging.

Legend has it that as the boards separated beneath his feet, Holmes cried out,

"I am Jack!"

Some of the spectators averted their gaze and two people fainted. The body's movement gradually ceased. Fifteen minutes later, two doctors checked for a pulse, listened to Holmes' chest, and pronounced the man dead. The crowd scattered, and while the body hung for an additional quarter hour, several prison officials and policemen filed by to view the sight.

The body was lowered onto a truck like so much dirty laundry, but officials had a difficult time separating the rope from Holmes' neck because it had cut so deeply into his flesh. Though Rotan pleaded with him to do so, Perkins refused to cut the rope off. Finally, it was removed and the hood lifted from Holmes' head. His face was swollen and pur-

**The strength of thirteen men was required to move Holmes'
cement-filled coffin from the vault to the open grave.
(*Philadelphia Inquirer;* May 9, 1896; Courtesy
the Free Library of Philadelphia).**

ple and his neck was broken. Rotan stood by to make sure that Holmes'

wishes were fulfilled and to assure that no autopsy was performed.

When Rotan was asked what Holmes had written to him just before

his death, he replied, "I have not gone over them yet, but I understand

that they are mostly directions to his attorneys to keep up the effort to

prove his innocence of murder."

Asked if Holmes wanted that search to continue, Rotan replied,

"He does, and he believes he will one day be successful. So do I." As to any funds left by Holmes to further that effort, Rotan replied, "He did not leave any with me – not one cent."

Undertaker J. J. O'Rourke arrived just before noon with a wagon containing an ordinary pine box. He took the body back to his business where he placed a slightly larger box in the back of the wagon. He and his assistants quickly mixed the cement and placed a layer several inches deep in the box. Into this bed of mortar, Holmes' body was placed, dressed exactly as he had been when he strode to his death. They placed a silk scarf over his face and filled the box entirely with cement. The lid was nailed down securely, and the wagon began its journey to Holy Cross Cemetery in Delaware County.

It was almost two o'clock when the undertakers arrived at the cemetery. There was some delay as the graveyard's superintendent awaited direct orders from his superiors to allow Holmes to rest in his garden. The coffin was temporarily moved to a nearby mausoleum-type vault. It took seven men to lift the coffin from the wagon and set it on the cold cement.

At around five o'clock, the wagon reached the spot in which the murderer would be interred. It took thirteen men, now, to drag the coffin from the vault toward the yawning grave several yards away. A group of reporters covering the burial came to assist, and finally, with thirteen men pushing and shoving the coffin, they inched it to the edge of the ten-foot-deep grave. But as the box was aimed into the hole, the men lost control of its descent.

It landed upside down in the bottom of the grave.

Someone remarked that this must be the hands of fate, giving Holmes the just reward of facing hell for all eternity. As darkness fell, only two detectives remained to stand vigil through the night to guarantee the body was not disturbed.

∾

The following morning, a two-foot layer of cement was dumped on top of the coffin before the remaining earth was shoveled into the hole.

Due to his notoriety, Holmes' death was recorded in red ink in the ledger by Registry Clerk Theodore M. Carr. The certificate of death for "Herman W. Mudgett, alias H. H. Holmes" was signed by Benjamin F. Butcher, M.D.

The cause of death?

"Hanging according to law."

"The importance of studying [Holmes] is to note the gradual steps that led him to his fate, which he probably never intended. He gradually gets accustomed to doing things, and forgets the feeling of the community."

Dr. Arthur MacDonald

(19th Century Criminologist)

Chapter Sixteen

Entry to an individual cell at Moyamensing required the unlocking of two separate doors. The first door, which contained no window, opened to a small space in which a person could sit and chat with an inmate without physically entering his cell. All daily requirements of food, water, and personal hygiene could be accomplished without anyone ever entering the cell itself. The second door, the one that actually opened into the room itself, had an open window with bars so that the prisoner could see who was present. Sounds from outside were drastically reduced and muffled by the dead space between the two portals.

After Holmes was moved to the first tier, the outer door was left open so the guards could keep an eye on Holmes to make sure he couldn't commit suicide. Isolated in his cold, lonely cell, Holmes saw very few people...his watchers, of course, as well as the priests and his attorneys. However, Holmes received regular visits from one other man, a criminologist from Washington, Dr. Arthur MacDonald.

The Bertillon System, a series of facial measurements and skull size, was used at that time to evaluate prisoners. The system was developed by Alphonse Bertillon, chief of criminal investigations in Paris in 1880. The method, known as anthropometry, evaluated a person based on measurements of head and body, tattoos, scars, and personality. The data was developed into a formula that would apply

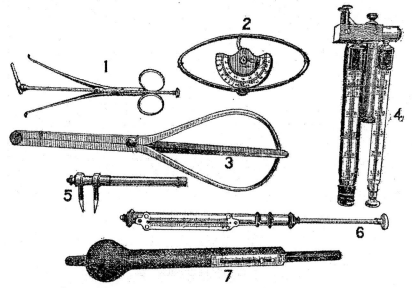

The tools Dr. MacDonald used to assess Holmes' sanity.

1. **Palameter**
2. **Hand-grasp Measure**
3. **Cranlometer**
4. **Thermaesthesfometer**
5. **Aesthesiometer**
6. **Temple algometer**
7. **Palm algometer**

(Courtesy the Library of Congress)

to only one person and would never change. In a very short time, the Bertillon System was being used in America and Britain, as well.

Predictably, the system was proven to be unreliable, since any two officers could come up with slightly different measurements on the same individual. The results also were skewed by age. After fingerprinting was developed, anthropometry was abandoned when the fingerprints of a Kansas man named Will West contradicted his Bertillon results. Following Holmes' conviction, a frequent visitor to his cell was federal criminologist Dr. Arthur MacDonald. MacDonald employed this method when he studied Holmes in hopes of gaining some glimmer of knowledge about the killer's motivations, hoping to enlighten future investigations. MacDonald also traveled extensively to interview people who had known Holmes before and during his criminal life. The criminologist prefaces his findings in this way,

"The intellectual education of a man at least fills his mind with subjects calculated to do him good. They do not tend to crime. But, of course, it is the moral side of education that has to do with the study of the criminal. It shows the importance of good habits, which the criminal seldom has. His life is irregular. He is a wanderer, from sociological necessity, and his wandering spirit leads to a feeling of irresponsibility. *A man among strangers is liable to regard them as, in a manner, enemies.*

"A common characteristic of the criminal is his vanity – the effect his crimes are liable to have on the community – and [Holmes] was no exception to this rule. Some criminals when performing a bloody act go into a sort of spasm, and after they have killed their victim hack him to pieces, and then lie down through exhaustion and sleep right by the side of the body until they are arrested.

"The antecedents and early training of [Holmes] will not account for his subsequent career in crime. The careful reader of the letters of his professors and classmates will have revealed to him the character of [Holmes] in both his strong and weak points. It will be seen that his entrée into crime was of a gradual nature. He began in his university life to manifest in embryo from time to time those characteristics which when small are not criminal, but when increased in their quantity become so detrimental to society that we rightly call them criminal.

"The following study of [Holmes] was made after several interviews with the murderer in his cell. A scientific study of him with instruments of precision of the latest design and also a psychological and sociological investigation of his character are presented. Although convicted of murder, he was not a murderer by nature, for he was too much of a coward, and so resorted to poison in extreme circumstances. It is easy to see how his medical knowledge and experience were utilized in carrying out his criminal designs.

"His chief abnormality is a psychological one. He is a reprobate liar. He had a selfish conscience. That is, when he was wronged he felt it (many criminals are very sensitive on this point). But in wrongdoing others he was willfully made obtuse by his overt acts. He was a deceiver by nature; and this, coupled with his greed for money, gradually led him into serious acts.

"But [Holmes] was effeminate in nature, and when taking human life he used an effeminate method, poisoning. Throughout the history of crime this has been woman's method. It is evident from the letters that his greed for money, with little or no aversion to deceive, and his poverty gradually led him on. Poverty is often an occasion but not a cause of a great deal of wrongdoing.

"His strong impulse to deception and greed was the hereditary side of his character; the degree to which he developed them into criminality depended upon his environment.

"In reply to the remark that it was temporarily assumed that [Holmes] might be guilty of some of the crimes he was accused of, the prisoner made the following statements:

Holmes: "I did not deny my guilt for several reasons; people would not believe me even if I told the truth. My counsel will tell you the reasons. I am preparing my affairs with a view that I am to be executed. I prefer it to imprisonment for life. If I were not executed the insurance companies would make an example of me. I am accused of seventeen murders, and the three insisted upon are shown to be false, how can any one [sic] believe me guilty of the others? I lived in Chicago ten years and had a good reputation."

(That statement is only partially correct. Holmes, in the end, had anything *but* a good reputation. That is why he had to leave town.)

MacDonald: "When told that criminals feared death more than other people and preferred imprisonment for life, he said he must be an exception; he was almost tempted to make a false confession in order to hang.

"When I inserted an instrument in his mouth to measure the height of his palate he said, as if afraid, 'Don't choke me.'

The first instrument MacDonald used on Holmes was the kymographion which supposedly measured "the effects of mental and emotional states upon the movements of the chest." MacDonald continues: "Actors locate the seat of the emotion they simulate in their chest.

THE KYMOGRAPHION RECORD.

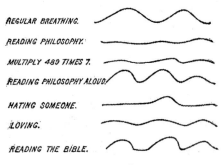

REGULAR BREATHING.

READING PHILOSOPHY.

MULTIPLY 489 TIMES 7.

READING PHILOSOPHY ALOUD.

HATING SOMEONE.

LOVING.

READING THE BIBLE.

Kymographion
(Courtesy the Library of Congress)

The kymographion was very similar to the modern polygraph machine in that the movements of the subject's chest were scratched on smoked paper by a small bamboo point. With every breath the bamboo sliver was raised and then lowered by exhaling, which created a wave-like line on the paper. MacDonald states that when asked if he had killed the Pitezel children, "[Holmes'] eyes bulged out, he turned red, and could say nothing."

In subsequent examinations, MacDonald noted a "depression on left side of skull at bregma [the front of the head], due to fall of a brick at the age of 31."

MacDonald's next observation was that Holmes' sexual organs were unusually small.

"He complained of being troubled with strabismus [a disorder of vision due to a deviation from normal orientation of one or both eyes so that both cannot be directed at the same object at the same time; crossed eyes, *Webster's New Universal Unabridged Dictionary,* copyright Barnes and Noble, 1996] from childhood; said his mother was an epileptic; that he was not nervous, but at present felt a little nervous.

"He had lived with a professor, who was his best friend, and who was at that time demonstrator of anatomy. He did not go to college, but graduated from the medical school. He added he was also a graduate in pharmacy. He would send all he had to say to his former

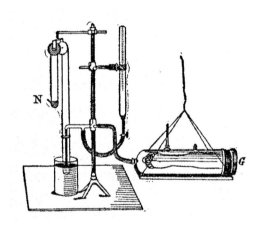

Plethysmograph
(Courtesy the Library of Congress)

professor (he did not do it), to whom I could write. He did not like to tell all on account of his domestic troubles, which had not been entered into. He admitted that he was married more than once.

"Antecedents and childhood: One who knew his family well says in a letter: '...inasmuch as [Holmes] and his parents were frequently attendants upon my father's preaching, and as he attended the district school taught by my wife's sister, and as his wife, and part of the time himself, were in the employ of an uncle of mine, I have a definite knowledge of his youth.

"'His people were very upright, God-fearing citizens, living in a quiet, secluded section of the country. There is no trace of open immorality or vice in the family history for at least three generations of which I have any knowledge. I am intimately acquainted with several cousins, and they are all upright to me.

"'As a boy, [Holmes] was a quiet, studious, faithful lad, with refined tastes, not caring to join to any extent the rude and rough games of his companions at school, and easily standing as the best scholar in his class. He was a general favorite with the mothers in that community, because he was such a well-behaved lad. In his youth he was predisposed to a religious life; was a faithful, painstaking student of the Scriptures, and rather excelled in his Sunday school class, and later in his Bible class, and my recollection is that he took an active part in the weekly prayer meetings and was known as a religious youth.'"

Letter from his first wife: "In regard to his childhood days I can not say much, as I did not know much of him until he was 17 years old. I always felt that he was pleasant in disposition, tender-hearted, much more so than people in general. He was of a very determined mind, at the same time quite considerate of others' comfort and welfare. In 1881 he was at [Burlington,

Vermont], for the year, and in the spring of 1882 he started for the university, and, as far as I knew, was doing quite well. I returned to [New Hampshire] the spring before he was to graduate, and have known very little of him since, but he has always been called smart, well educated, and a man of refined ways. Before attending the medical school he taught school several terms and was very successful – as much so as teachers in general – and when the story came out people who had always known him said, 'We can not believe this. [Holmes] would not have the heart or courage to do anything so terrible.' But of course he has worked himself up to it little by little, and I think, having done some little wrong, he had been driven to a greater one for a cover, and each one growing worse, of course it is easy or more easy to go in the wrong after the first few steps."

Letter from former professor: "It is true that while a student here he was for a year or two under my roof, but not in any intimate relations with me as to justify him as looking upon me as his best friend; if so, his friends must be few. However, I am very sorry for him, even although [sic] he himself may be the direct cause of his present miseries and threatening punishments. He told me a few months ago, when I visited him in prison, that he and another classmate had worked up a scheme to defraud an insurance company a few months after they graduated in 1884 from the medical department here, but that the scheme fell through because of his friend's death, which occurred within a year after he graduated. I do not know whether he graduated in pharmacy or not. He certainly did not take that course here, as I find he was never entered as a pharmacy student. He may have taken the degree elsewhere, but if he did it was after he graduated in medicine, as he made no claim to having had a pharmacy course when he was here.

"There were several things that occurred when he was here as a student that in the light of subsequent events show him to have been even at that time well practiced in criminal habits. Although he was married and had his wife here for a time doing work as a dressmaker and assisting in supporting himself and her, yet he got into trouble by showing some attention to a grass widow, who was engaged in the business of hair dressing." [A grass widow can be several things...a woman who is separated, divorced, or lives apart from her husband; a woman whose husband is away from home frequently or for a long time; a discarded mistress; a woman who has borne an illegitimate child: *Websters New Universal Unabridged Dictionary*, copyright Barnes & Noble, 1996]. This woman made some complaints to the faculty during the latter part of his senior year, and the stories that she told, had they been confirmed, would have prevented him from graduating. But I had no reason to doubt his word at that time, and his friends lied for him so vigorously that I was wholly deceived and defended him before the faculty, and he was permitted to graduate. On the afternoon of commencement day he came to me on his own accord, with his diploma in his hand, and said: 'Doctor those things are true that that woman said about me.' This was the first positive evidence that I had received up until that time that the fellow was a scoundrel, and I took occasion to tell him so at that time. I subsequently learned, however, that he had made two attempts to enter my house in the character of a burglar, and also that he had while occupying a room in a portion of my house attempted to force a drawer in my library in which I had been in the habit of keeping valuables. Three months after he had graduated in medicine, and knowing full well what opinion I entertained of him, he wrote me asking for a recommendation to assist him in getting an appointment as a missionary to Africa. This I was satisfied he did simply from the spirit of devilishness, and not that he had an serious intentions of carrying out such a purpose. These and many little incidents that I might relate to you, some of them personal experiences of my own with him, and others that have been told me by members of my family, serve to further illustrate these traits in his character, but they are all of the same nature as those that I have mentioned."

Another professor wrote to MacDonald, saying "Personally, I can not recall [Holmes'] features. I only remember that he failed to pass in my work and that I voted against his graduation."

Testimony of His Classmates

Classmate #1: "Myself and family lived in the house with [Holmes] and his family almost one school year. His family consisted of a wife and one child (a boy about 4 years old). His wife was a very pleasant woman and willing to make any sacrifice that she might help him along in his course. She finally went out to work and gave him her earnings. She was subject to convulsions of some kind, and while at work he gave her such quantities of bromide that her face broke out very badly. Every one thought it too bad for her. He must have been in very straitened [sic] circumstances, for he managed different ways of getting along. I remember he built a barn for a widow woman who was studying medicine in the homeopathy department at that time. She told me how [Holmes] beat her on the barn. He was very dishonest and tricky any place you found him. He would borrow everything of the students that he could to save himself buying. I have no picture of [Holmes]. Would never have recognized him by his picture in the papers. At that time he had a rather slender face, wore chin whiskers, not considered good looking, but I remember he had treacherous-looking eyes. Another piece of his wife's economy was to borrow our sewing machine and completely turn a coat for him. He was not a graduate in pharmacy to my knowledge."

Classmate #2: "It happened that [Holmes] acted as steward of a boarding house (only table boarding). It was his duty to keep the places at table filled with students and collect the money weekly. My recollection of him is quite distinct. None of the boys ever knew much of him (further than that he admitted himself to be married), or had much to do with him. His associations with his fellow students amounted to but little, because of his way of living. He had no money, at least that is what he always said. For his meals he conducted the club, while he slept at Dr. H's house. (Dr. H was the demonstrator of anatomy in the university.) This brought him to the boarding house only at mealtime. The money was collected by [Holmes] regularly every Saturday evening. He was, as I remember, always punctual in performing his duties, and also regular at his meals. Even now I can see him sitting at the lower, dark end of the long table, saying but little and laughing very seldom. He was a remarkable taciturn disposition, apparently indifferent to his surroundings, coldly methodical, unresponsive to humor, and very brief in his statements. His topics of conversation were mainly concerning Dr. H's operations upon his private patients. [Holmes], as I have said, slept at Dr. H's house. He always accompanied Dr. H upon his night trips. We students, remarking the thing, always thought that H's quietness was due to his rest being broken and irregular, having always to hitch up the horse for the Dr.'s use, perhaps accompany him, and then stable the horse upon the Dr.'s return. I remember once of asking a medical student how [Holmes] answered up in his 'quiz.' The answer I got was that he was not reliable or exact in his knowledge."

Chapter Seventeen

HOLMES CURSE & SUPERSTITIONS

The horoscope given for the date and time of Holmes' birth proved surprisingly accurate. The alignment of the planets promised life changes, mystery, extraordinary conduct, a flighty, emotional temperament, and a fickle character. There were also unmistakable signs of foreboding – disaster, business failures, and promised misfortune for those who associated with him.

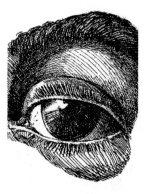

A sketch of Holmes' "evil eye." (*The Chicago Daily News;* May 10, 1896; Courtesy the Abraham Lincoln Presidential Library).

There was a great deal of talk during Holmes' trial of all these portents, but they weren't given much credibility until tragedy began to strike those involved in his trial and execution. Then the citizens began to murmur of "something magnetically evil about the man whose murders have shocked the world."

Dr. William K. Mattern, a medical examiner who was an important witness in Holmes' trial, was stricken with a fatal case of food poisoning shortly after Holmes' execution. Coroner Ashbridge was taken so seriously ill his friends and family genuinely feared for his life. Another key player who hovered near death for a while was Judge Arnold. Frank Geyer also fell ill and was incapacitated for a year.

Moyamensing Superintendent Perkins committed suicide, and Holmes' Chicago attorney died

H. H. Holmes

Herman Webster Mudgett, alias Dr. Henry Howard Holmes... a real-life Jekyll & Hyde. (Courtesy the Abraham Lincoln Presidential Library).

suddenly. Peter Cigrand, father of Emeline, was critically burned in a gas explosion just as he prepared to go to Philadelphia to witness the hanging. And William Shoemaker, one half of the team who defended Holmes during his trial, met with professional disaster and was disbarred.

Fr. Henry McPake, who ventured out late one night, was found dead in the church's backyard and the cause of death listed as uremia. This only meant that there were no obvious reasons for his death, so it was assumed to be from natural causes. An argument against natural

219

causes, though, were the bruises about his head, and the fact that his watch and other valuables were missing. His clothing was disarranged, there were boot marks near the body, and bloodstains on the fence.

A fire at the Fidelity Mutual Life Insurance Company's building destroyed only the office of O. LeForrest Perry before being extinguished. Several checks and all of his valuable papers were lost in the blaze. The only items unscathed by the fire were the warrant for Holmes' arrest, which was displayed in a frame over his desk, and two cabinet photographs of the dead killer. The frame in which the warrant resided was burned up, the glass was cracked in several places, but the warrant was undamaged except for a couple of spots of slight discoloration.

Linford Biles, the jury foreman at Holmes' trial lived in a house next to a cemetery. When a heavy wind blew through, the telephone and telegraph wires that crossed above his house would touch and throw off sparks. He had extinguished a fire on his roof shortly before he was

In this unmarked area of Holy Cross Cemetery, Herman W. Mudgett, alias Dr. H. H. Holmes, lies ten feet below ground, encased in five feet of concrete. (Snavely Collection)

chosen to serve on Holmes' jury. Within a year after Holmes' execution, Biles was once again atop his roof to put out yet another fire. He was electrocuted by one of the wires and fell dead to the ground. The shock was estimated to be enough to kill a dozen men. His left hand scorched, foot scarred, and forehead discolored, it appeared he had inadvertently stepped on the end of a live wire on the wet roof.

Finally, in 1910, Pat Quinlan committed suicide. His friends said that Quinlan had been haunted by his malicious career as Holmes' toady and, because of that, suffered insomnia. Those close to him had been expecting his suicidal act for a while. Observers of the news speculated that perhaps Holmes had come back and taken the only person who could reveal, in full, his heinous crimes.

Because Holmes remained alive for fifteen minutes with a broken neck, notion began to circulate that his was an evil spirit that would not die.

The lot where the Castle was located remained empty for many years until a U.S. Post Office was built on the site in 1938. Many in the area still remembered the stories of Holmes' castle -- or the tales from people who claimed to hear moaning and crying sounds coming from the grounds. There were those who stated that the ghosts of Holmes' victims did not rest in peace. The ground was believed to be tainted by the death and bloodshed that had occurred on the spot, and the over-grown lot was largely shunned and avoided. Most longtime residents would go out of their way to walk on the other side of the street.

Even after the post office was constructed on the site where so much torture and murder took place, strange things were still reported. Passersby who walked their dogs past the new building claimed the animals would often pull away from it, barking and whining at something they could see or sense. What agitated the dogs and was so terrifyingly real to them, however, remained invisible to their human masters.

The Englewood Post Office stands where Holmes' Castle once thrived. (Snavely Collection)

In addition, postal workers in the building had their own encounters, often telling of strange sounds and feelings they could not easily explain. The location was certainly ripe for a haunting, and if the stories can be believed, it was, and is still taking place.

Epilogue

In the spring of 1860, the turmoil that threatened the Union must have seemed far removed from the tiny hamlet of Gilmanton Corners, New Hampshire, a town best known for being the birth site of that infamous bestseller, *Peyton Place*. Grace Metalious wrote the torrid novel on a manual typewriter at her dining room table in Gilmanton in the 1950's. When Grace died of cirrhosis at the age of thirty-nine, she was laid to rest in the Smith Meeting House Cemetery in Gilmanton. In fact, that is the first thing most locals boast about to visitors. Few of them recognize the name of native son, Herman Webster Mudgett, America's most prolific and least-known serial killer.

The mostly-academic community had sprung up around Gilmanton Academy, a boarding school for boys. Down the road about eight miles was Gilmanton Iron Works, but the two communities existed quite separately from each other. To outsiders on whom the territorial nuances were lost, the entire area was known simply as Gilmanton.

Gilmanton Academy still stands, nestled among lush, gently rolling hills. A white clapboard church fronts the east entrance of the circular drive leading to the school, which now houses the town offices of Gilmanton Corners. And directly across the street, facing the academy, is a white frame house with a green roof. It looks different now from what it did a hundred and fifty years ago. Gone is the little porch that sheltered the front door, as are the second-floor dormer windows. A

223

two-car garage has been added in the rear, and utility lines anchor the old house to modern amenities.

In this house, on May 16, 1860, America's most prolific serial killer, Herman Webster Mudgett, alias Dr. H. H. Holmes, was born. A year later, the first shots were fired on Fort Sumpter, initiating the bloodiest war in American history. At the end of the Civil War, as Lee surrendered to Grant at Appomattox, Herman was just a year away from starting first grade. The Ku Klux Klan took hold in the South and the first assassination of a U.S. president snuffed the life of Abraham Lincoln, stunning the nation.

While the killer studied medicine in 1881, a second president, James Garfield was shot to death. By the time Holmes was executed in Philadelphia, the last of the American natives were being forced onto reservations in Oklahoma Territory. The slaughter of these indigenous people and the 850,000 Americans killed during the Civil War may have blunted the impact of 300 murders by one man.

It is only certain that Mudgett/Holmes' incredible story got lost in history and is only now emerging from obscurity.

Afterword

In the classic cartoon series "Rocky & Bullwinkle," there is a character named Mr. Peabody. Mr. Peabody is a professor at Wattsamatta U., and he has perfected a device he calls the "Way-Back Machine;" basically a time-travel device.

I have often heard people quizzed about the one place or person in history that they would visit should time travel become a reality. For this writer, there is no contest: 1894 Chicago, 63rd & Wallace. To wander around the Castle and see for myself the structure's anomalies; the room split in half horizontally, the maze into the bathroom, all the different passageways, secret stairs, and especially the "hanging" room. Just exactly what that label might have meant has kept me awake many nights, my mind searching to solve the riddle of Dr. Holmes' Castle. In visiting this infamous building, maybe I could glean the purpose of the Castle's strang amenities.

And how amazing it would be to come face to face (with mace in hand, of course) with this man whose story has dominated eight years of my life.

Time travel not being a reality, I must content myself with speculation about many aspects of Holmes' life.

But I'll never give up hope of locating Mr Peabody's "Way-Back Machine."

BIBLIOGRAPHY

The following newspapers for the period June 1894-May 1896:

Philadelphia Public Ledger

Philadelphia Inquirer

Philadelphia Times

Chicago Tribune

Chicago Inter Ocean

Chicago Times-Herald

New York Times

New York World

New York Herald

The Boston Globe

Chicago by Gaslight, by Richard Lindberg; (Chicago: Academy Chicago Publishers, 1986)

Bloodletters and Badmen, by Jay Robert Nash; (New York: M. Evans and Company, Inc., 1995)

Depraved, by Harold Schechter; (New York: Pocket Books, 1994)

Gem of the Prairie, by Herbert Asbury; (Dekalb, IL, Northern Illinois University Press, 1986)

The Torture Doctor, by David Franke, (New York: Hawthorne Books, Inc., 1975)

The Girls of Nightmare House, (New York: Fawcett Publications, 1955)

The Trial of Herman W. Mudgett, (trial transcript), (Philadelphia: George T. Bisel, 1897)

The Holmes-Pitezel Case, by Detective Frank P. Geyer; (Philadelphia: Publisher's Union, 1896)

Holmes' Own Story, by Herman W. Mudgett, alias H. H. Holmes, (Philadelphia: Burk & McFetridge Co., 1895)

The Holmes Castle, by Robert L. Corbitt, (Chicago: Corbitt & Morrison, 1895)

Holmes, the Arch Fiend, or: A Carnival of Crime, (Cincinnati: Barclay & Co., ca1896

United States Education Report 1893-1894; Arthur MacDonald, specialist in the Bureau of Education; Federal Publication

Index

Detroit, Michigan 19, 95, 99, 126, 127, 128, 135, 136
Dietsch, Philip 117
Divorce 27, 28, 49, 50
Dr. Wight 4, 5
Dugan, Deputy Coroner 80
Dwight, Illinois 54

E

Edison, Thomas 60
Elasticity Determinator 40
Englewood 23, 24, 28, 46, 54, 222
Eschler, Tom 7
  Gant House 10, 11

F

Fidelity Mutual Life Insurance Company 78, 220
  Ben Pitezel's Policy 66, 69, 109, 178
    Premium Telegraphed 79, 85
  L. G. Fouse 79, 80, 197
  O. LaForrest Perry 79
  Philadelphia Office 79
  St. Louis Office 78
    George B. Stadden 78
Fort Worth, Texas vii, 58, 59, 63, 65, 67, 69, 87, 92
Fort Worth National Bank 92

G

Gary, William 83
Georgiana Yoke 64, 104, 108, 158
  ABC Copier Company 42, 65, 102
  Denver, Colorado 65, 67, 87, 171
Geyer, Frank 115, 116, 162, 197, 219
  Annie Gaskins 115
  Daughter Esther 116
  Wife Martha 116
Gilmanton Academy 13, 223
Gilmanton Corners 3, 6, 223
Gilmanton Iron Works 223
Graham, George S. 114

H

Harrington, Lawrence 101
Hedgepeth, Marion 68, 70, 71, 79, 83, 85
  Prairie Home, Missouri 70
  The Handsome Bandit 71
Holmes, H. H. vii, viii, 1, 2, 12, 16, 21, 22, 23, 25, 26, 27, 28, 29, 30, 31, 32, 33, 34, 35, 36, 39, 40, 41, 42, 43, 45, 46, 47, 48, 49, 50, 51, 52, 53, 54, 55, 56, 57, 58, 59, 60, 61, 62, 63, 64, 65, 66, 67, 68, 71, 73, 74, 78, 79, 80, 81, 82, 83, 85, 86, 87, 88, 90, 91, 92, 93, 94, 95, 96, 98, 99, 100, 101, 102, 103, 104, 105, 107, 108, 109, 110, 111, 113, 114, 115, 117, 118, 119, 122, 124, 125, 126, 127, 128, 129, 130, 131, 132, 135, 136, 138, 139, 140, 141, 142, 144, 145, 146, 147, 148, 149, 150, 151, 152, 153, 154, 155, 157, 158, 159, 162, 163, 164, 165, 166, 167, 168, 169, 170, 171, 172, 173, 180, 181, 182, 185, 186, 188, 189, 190, 191, 192, 193, 194, 195, 196, 197, 198, 199, 200, 201, 202, 203, 204, 205, 206, 207, 208, 209, 210, 211, 212, 213, 215, 216, 217, 218, 219, 220, 221, 222, 224
  Arraignment 184
  Arrests 16, 48, 57, 64, 73, 86, 112, 113, 114, 177, 187, 220
  Burial 188, 196, 203
    Holy Cross Cemetery 203
    J. J. O'Rourke 203
    Registry Clerk 204
    Theodore M. Carr 204
  Burial Plans 196
  Confession 1, 16, 104, 171, 172, 175, 187, 189, 191, 192, 210

I

Indianapolis, Indiana 87, 91, 119, 122, 124, 125, 127, 136, 137
  Circle House 91, 93, 123, 124, 125
    Ackelow 124, 125
    Chambermaid Caroline Klausmann 125
  Circle Park Hotel 91, 92, 124
    Mrs. Rodius 124
  Irvington House 94, 95, 136, 139
    Dr. Barnhill 137, 140
    Dr. Byram 140
    Dr. Thompson 136, 137
    Mr. Brown 68, 136
    Oscar Kettenbach 137
    Walter Jenny 137
  Stubbins Hotel 87
Insurance Scam 71
Insurance Scheme 14, 17
Irvington, Indiana 94, 95
  Cottage 95, 96, 129, 136

J

Jackson, Mississippi 58
Jeweler Davis 46
Jones, A. L. 40

K

Keeley Institute 54

L

LaSalle Medical School 56
Lovering, Clara 13, 14, 16, 27, 103, 104, 105, 106, 174

M

MacDonald, Dr. Arthur 206
  Case Study of Holmes 2, 32, 34, 43, 47, 85, 86, 108, 115, 117, 118, 129, 140, 141, 144, 146, 149, 159, 171, 190, 218, 221
  Letter from First Wife 212
  Letter from Former Professor 211, 213
  Testimony of His Classmates 215
Mattern, Dr. 80, 81
Minneapolis 19, 27
Minnie Williams 57, 58, 69, 86, 94
  Boston Conservatory of Music and Elocution 58
Missippi 57, 58, 60
Momence, Illinois 61
Mooers Fork, New York 17
Moyamensing Prison 1, 4, 14, 68, 114, 157, 168, 193, 195
Mudgett, Herman W. 1, 102, 147, 165, 167, 204
  Aliases 86, 99, 126
    A. C. Hayes 88, 118
    Alexander E. Cook 88
    D. T. Pratt 66
    Edward Hatch 57, 125, 126
    George H. Howell 128
    Harry (Henry) Gordon 57, 59, 60, 91, 93, 94
    Henry Howard Holmes 22, 219
    J. A. Judson 101
    Mr. Hall 101
    Robert Phelps 56
  Castle 29, 31, 32, 33, 34, 35, 36, 37, 38, 40, 41, 42, 43, 45, 46, 47, 48, 50, 53, 54, 55, 56, 57, 58, 59, 60, 63, 64, 66, 86, 126, 140, 141, 142, 143, 145, 180, 181, 184, 221, 222
  Children 2, 3, 72, 80, 81, 82, 85, 87, 88, 91, 93, 94, 99, 100, 101, 116, 117, 118, 119, 122, 124, 125, 126, 129, 133, 134, 137, 138, 140, 157, 162, 163, 164, 185, 186, 187, 199, 210
  Lucy Holmes 28
  Robert Lovering Mudgett 16, 103
  Medical School 14, 20, 53, 180, 211, 213
  Memoirs viii, 12, 14, 20, 34, 57, 104, 105, 113

AN HISTORICAL TIMELINE SPANNING THE LIFE OF
HERMAN WEBSTER MUDGETT, ALIAS DR. H. H. HOLMES

May 16, 1860	March 12, 1861	March 9, 1865	May 10, 1869
Herman W. Mudgett is born in Gilmanton, N.H.		Herman starts school and bullies drop him at the feet of Dr. Wight's skeleton	Herman is disappointed in his new watch; he and Tom take revenge on teacher
Abraham Lincoln receives the Republican nomination for president	Fort Sumpter fires on Charleston, S.C., beginning the Civil War	Gen. Robert E. Lee surrenders to Gen. Ulysses S. Grant at Appomadox	Golden railroad spike completes the nation's first transcontinental railroad line

Oct. 8, 1871	March 10, 1876	June 25, 1876	Dec. 15, 1877
While Herman and Tom (his only close childhood friend) explore the Gant house, Tom falls to his death	Herman graduates from the Academy	Herman teaches school Gilmanton	An ambitious Herman sets his sights on medical school
Chicago fire kills 300 people and devastates the city	Alexander Graham Bell successfully tests the first telephone	Gen. George Armstrong Custer is defeated by the Sioux at Little Big Horn	Thomas Edison applies for a patent on his first phonograph invention

Oct. 21, 1879	July 2, 1881	May 25, 1883	April 22, 1889
On July 4, 1878, Herman marries Clara Lovering	Herman attends medical school at the University of Michigan, financing his education with insurance frauds	A year later, Herman graduates from medical school with the class of 1884	Now Dr. H. H. Holmes, the killer has married Myrta and become the father of Lucy. The Holmes' Castle is almost finished
Thomas Edison successfully tests his first practical light bulb; it burns for 13 hours	President Garfield is shot; dies 2 1/2 months later of blood poisoning	Brooklyn Bridge is completed, linking the NY boroughs of Manhattan & Brooklyn	At high noon, 200,000 settlers rush into Indian Territory to claim land

237

Dec. 29, 1890	May 1, 1893	1893	Jan. 17, 1894
The Holmes' Castle is completed; Ben Pitezel and Pat Quinlan are now employees of Holmes. He kills the Conner family	Holmes is playing host to thousands of visitors; defrauds investors in his water-to-gas machine scam; he kills Emeline Cigrand	Holmes' creditors begin to close in; he kills the Williams sisters & confiscates their Fort Worth property	Holmes marries Georgiana Yoke using the last name of Howard; kills brother of Williams sisters for insurance payoff
Wounded Knee Massacre becomes the last battle between whites and Native Americans	The great Chicago World's Fair (The Columbian Exposition) opens to commemorate 400th anniversary of Christopher Columbus' discovery of America.	A growing credit shortage fuels a substantial depression in the U.S.	The depression continues; Jacob Coxey leads a protest in Washington, D.C. and is arrested for walking on the grass

Jan.- Apr., 1894	May 21, 1894	July 19, 1894	August, 1894
Holmes, Georgiana, & Pitezel are in Fort Worth; gain title to Williams sisters' land & begins second "castle." Forced to leave town after stealing some horses	The threesome arrives in St. Louis & Holmes buys drug store; pulls fraud on suppliers	Holmes is arrested & shares a jail cell with Marion Hedgepeth, who sets Holmes up with attorney Jeptha Howe	Pitezel opens patent office in Philadelphia; a month later, inventor Eugene Smith finds Pitezel's body

The country continues to struggle with financial depression

239

September, 1894	October, 1894	November, 1894	June, 1894
Alice identifies her father's body; Holmes leaves Philadelphia with Alice, Nettie, & Howard Pitezel	Holmes kills all three Pitezel children	Holmes visits his family in Gilmanton; he & Carrie are arrested in Boston & extradicted to Philadelphia	Holmes is arraigned on insurance fraud; Det. Frank Geyer leaves Philadelphia in search of Pitezel children

240

July, 1895	Sept. 12, 1895	Nov. 2, 1895	May 7, 1896
Geyer finds the bodies of all three Pitezel children; Chicago police begin the search of Holmes' Castle	Holmes arraigned for murder of Ben Pitezel	Holmes convicted of murder	Holmes is hanged at Moyamensing Prison in Philadelphia; his body is buried in Holy Cross Cemetery

The day before Holmes' execution, the Supreme Court rules that it is permissible to maintain separate facilities for blacks – as long as these facilities are equal to those provided to whites. This is the legal basis for establishing segregation of school systems until it is reversed by Brown vs. Board of Education in 1954.

Printed in the United States
54580LVS00003B/118-312